Oxford Studies of Composers (22)

SWEELINCK

FRITS NOSKE

OXFORD UNIVERSITY PRESS

1988

Oxford University Press, Walton Street, Oxford OX2 6DP

Oxford New York Toronto
Delhi Bombay Calcutta Madras Karachi
Petaling Jaya Singapore Hong Kong Tokyo
Nairobi Dar es Salaam Cape Town
Melbourne Auckland

and associated companies in
Beirut Berlin Ibadan Nicosia

Oxford is a trade mark of Oxford University Press

British Library Cataloguing in Publication Data
Noske, Frits
Sweelinck.—(Oxford studies of composers; 22).
1. Sweelinck, Jan Pieterszoon, 1562–1621
2. Composers—Netherlands—Biography
I. Title
780'.92'4   ML410.S97
ISBN 0–19–315259–2

Library of Congress Cataloging in Publication Data
Noske, Frits, 1920–
Sweelinck/Frits Noske.
p. cm.—(Oxford studies of composers: 22)
Bibliography: p.
Includes index.
1. Sweelinck, Jan Peiterszoon, 1562–1621. 2. Composers—
Netherlands—Biography. I. Title. II. Series.
ML410.S97N73 1988 780'.92'4–dc 19 87–34501
ISBN 0–19–315259–2

Set by Cambrian Typesetters, Frimley, Camberley, Surrey.
Printed and bound in Great Britain
at the University Printing House, Oxford
by David Stanford
Printer to the University

PREFACE

No student of Sweelinck and his work can disregard the pioneering monograph of Bernard van den Sigtenhorst Meyer, published in two volumes shortly after the Second World War. Despite the author's outmoded analytical methods and limited knowledge of English, Italian, and German music of Sweelinck's time, his study contains a wealth of shrewd observations that are still valid today. Further, I recognize my debt to Alan Curtis, whose excellent work on the English elements in seventeenth-century Dutch composition has clarified many problems concerning Sweelinck's keyboard style within the musical landscape of his time. I also wish to thank Dr Annette Verhoeven-Kooij (Amsterdam), who graciously put at my disposal her manuscript of the still unpublished *Opera omnia*, vii, and, finally, Professor Michael Talbot (Liverpool), who most kindly assisted me by painstakingly correcting my English.

Airolo (Ticino)   F. N.
April 1987

CONTENTS

I

SWEELINCK AND THE RISE
OF AMSTERDAM

Among the great composers in the history of Western music, Jan·
Pieterszoon Sweelinck presents the exceptional case of a man
occupying only one post during his whole life: that of organist at the
Oude Kerk of Amsterdam. Moreover, his father as well as his son
Dirck served this church in the same capacity. The musical activities of
three generations of one family, spanning nearly a century (1564–
1652), thus coincides more or less with the spectacular rise of
Amsterdam from a relatively small trading centre to the economic
focus of the European continent. Therefore it may be useful to begin
this short study with a brief description of the town before and during
Sweelinck's time, the way in which it was ruled, and, more specifically,
its musical life.

Mentioned as a village in an official document dating from 1275,
Amsterdam must have obtained its municipal status shortly after 1300.
At that time most of its inhabitants were fishermen. However, in the
course of the next two and a half centuries, trade and, linked with this,
shipbuilding gradually grew in importance. Around 1550 Amsterdam
began to overtake other flourishing centres in the County of Holland,
such as Dordrecht, Leyden, and Haarlem. During the early years of
the Dutch insurrection against their overlord, King Philip II of Spain,
the town remained politically passive; it was only in 1578 that its
citizens deposed the Catholic magistracy and took the side of Prince
William of Orange (the so-called 'Alteration'). During the 1580s the
Republic of the United Provinces was founded, but the decisive factor
contributing to the future supremacy of Amsterdam was paradoxically
a military defeat: the siege and capture of Antwerp by the Spanish
army in 1585. The Dutch immediately reacted by closing Antwerp's
access to the sea, and so Amsterdam got rid of its main commercial
competitor. During the following sixty years the number of inhabitants
grew from c.30,000 to c.200,000; by 1650 the town had become a
mercantile metropolis, without rival on the continent. Many Protestant
immigrants settled within its walls: first, mainly Flemings refusing to

1

live under the rule of Philip II in the Southern Netherlands; later, after the turn of the century, inhabitants of central Europe who left their countries dominated by another champion of the Counter Reformation, the Habsburg Emperor.

The system by which most of the towns in the County of Holland were governed in the course of the fifteenth century was by the Dukes of Burgundy; as regards Amsterdam, it was the Duchess Mary, daughter of Charles the Bold, who granted the town freedom in the sphere of jurisdiction, as well as other privileges. The magistracy consisted of a number of burgomasters (in Sweelinck's time four) and a municipal 'parliament' (the *vroedschap*) of 30 to 40 members. As the latter body had only an advisory function, the burgomasters' power was virtually unlimited. It is a curious fact that this oligarchic system remained almost unchallenged until the end of the Republic (1795). The reason may have been that the citizens' pursuits paralleled those of the wealthy merchants who ruled the city. The greater part of the population was involved in trade and no conflicting interests separated the small merchants from the rich governors. Besides, unlike agricultural regions, mercantile communities allowed a remarkable social mobility, which was not restricted to the merchants proper; craftsmen and artists also profited from it, Sweelinck's career being a case in point.

The particularly tolerant social climate may be explained by mercenary motives, but it also arose from a humanist, Erasmian tradition. Calvinism had of course its fanatics, ministers as well as laymen; these, however, were kept in check by the magistrates. The latter strongly cared for social order; with institutions like old men's and women's homes, orphanages, and the *rasphuis*, a house of correction, Amsterdam was well ahead of its time. The religious tolerance is attested by the fact that by about 1650 the city housed no fewer than 30,000 Catholics, who held their services in so-called hidden churches (which nevertheless were known to every citizen). As membership of the Dutch Reformed Church was a condition for holding a public office, quite a number of people adhered to the privileged religion for purely opportunistic reasons. Thus the total of *de facto* Catholics may even have been higher.

The most spectacular achievement of the Amsterdam magistracy was the planning of the town's rapid enlargement during the first half of the seventeenth century. In Sweelinck's youth Amsterdam extended over little more than the area between the harbour and the river Amstel. Soon after the turn of the century, however, expansion

2

towards the south was taken in hand: three girdles of new canals, each forming a semicircle, ensured a harmonious architectonic development which was admired far beyond the country's borders, as it is still in our own time. Finally, after the fire that destroyed the old town hall, a new building of unparalleled magnificence was erected, standing on 13,000 wooden piles because of the softness of the soil. Since the early nineteenth century this monumental edifice has served as a royal palace.

As there is no Amsterdam musician of distinction traceable before Sweelinck, the town's early music history may seem a rather indifferent affair. Nevertheless, through the various visits of the Dukes of Burgundy and the Habsburg Emperors, who were always accompanied by their chapels, the citizens must have become acquainted with the music of the Franco-Flemish schools. There is evidence that the practice of music, albeit mainly non-polyphonic music, was well developed in the four churches: St Nicholas's Church, better known as the Oude Kerk (1334), St Catherine's Church (the Nieuwe Kerk, early sixteenth century), as well as two small parish churches (1347 and c.1450). In addition, the town housed no less than twenty-two monasteries and convents whose services undoubtedly accommodated a wide repertory of Gregorian chant. In this connection a significant fact may be noted: in 1561 the magistracy ordered the Louvain firm of Phalèse to print 200 copies of a book containing a local repertory, *Cantuale iuxta usum insignis ecclesiae Amstelredamensis*. It is particularly remarkable that as late as 1619 Sweelinck based one of his *Cantiones sacrae* on a melody taken from this collection (see the section on Latin motets in Chapter III). Polyphonic singing in church was introduced at the beginning of the sixteenth century, but very little is known about either this or the function of the organists. The possibility exists that pre-reformation 'concerts', as documented for St Bavo's Church in Haarlem, were also given in Amsterdam.

The 'Alteration' of 1578 put an abrupt end to the role of music in public worship, with the sole exception of monophonic psalm singing intoned by a precentor. The Calvinists not only rejected Gregorian chant and polyphonic music during the service, they also considered the organ a worldly instrument. The National Synod even went so far as to request the removal of organs from the churches. A fortunate circumstance prevented the implementation of this resolution, however: in almost all the Dutch towns joining the insurrection, either of their own volition or through being conquered, the churches with their organs became municipal property, administered by or on behalf of the

3

magistracy. Apart from the services held on Sundays, the buildings thus served worldly purposes, such as the public 'concerts' given once or twice a day by the organist, whose employer was the town, not the church. Organs became objects of local prestige, and many towns spent considerable sums on their restoration or the purchase of new instruments. Organists enjoyed a fairly high social reputation; their salaries, on the other hand, were rather low.

Nor was this the only involvement of the municipal authorities in musical life. They also appointed the town's carillonneur, whose popularity even exceeded that of the organist. In an age that happily lacked the mechanical noises of today, the sound of the bells, the most authentic music of the Netherlands, was heard in every corner of the town. As the repertory consisted almost exclusively of improvisations on secular and sacred tunes, very little of this music has been preserved. In addition, many towns including Amsterdam had their ensemble of *stadsmuzikanten*, a group of shawm and cornet players who, dressed in colourful livery, brightened festive events and solemnities with their music. They usually played on the flight of steps before the town hall or on the gallery of the church tower. Membership of this body being only a part-time occupation, several organists or carillonneurs also worked as town musicians. For that matter, the posts of organist and carillonneur were also often combined, especially in the small towns.

All in all, public music in the Dutch Republic seems to have been a rather parochial affair. Still, in a country where neither Church nor Court had anything to offer, the efforts of the local authorities to promote musical activities were most remarkable. While it is true that the magistrates could not emulate the patronage of princes and cardinals elsewhere in Europe, their role foreshadowed more or less the official support and stimulation of the Fine Arts in our modern society.

In contrast with the restricted domain of public music, which was exclusively instrumental, the practice of singing at home was widespread. The performance of sacred and secular compositions, such as motets, psalm settings, chansons, and madrigals, had a special place in domestic life. The family and their friends usually joined for this purpose after the midday meal. Many paintings reflect the Dutchman's love of music-making during the late sixteenth and seventeenth centuries. It should be noted, however, that painters emphasized the use of instruments, playing down the role of singing. The obvious reason for this is that an instrumentalist was a far more attractive subject to depict than a singer.

4

Out of domestic musical practice grew the institutions known as *collegia musica*, amateur 'clubs' for gentlemen (and occasionally ladies) who, guided by a professional musician, met at least once a week to make music, sacred as well as secular. Among its members there might have been persons belonging to the local magistracy; this perhaps explains the fact that in the course of the seventeenth century these small societies often became subsidized by the town.[1] Like Arnhem and Leeuwarden, Amsterdam already had its *collegium musicum* in the 1590s, and the greater part of Sweelinck's vocal output seems to have been written, directly or indirectly, for this group of amateur singers. Their vocal capacities were highly developed, as can be seen from the composer's scores. Apart from this, we know that Sweelinck also directed a consort of viols.

The lack of spectacular features in Dutch musical life could be compensated for only by particularly high artistic qualities. The case of Sweelinck proves that this was indeed possible.

The only important event in Sweelinck's life that is unconnected with Amsterdam was his birth. As we know from a poem by Jacobus Revius, the composer was born in Deventer, an important town in the east Netherlands belonging to the Hanseatic League. The following lines (in translation) comment on one of Sweelinck's portraits:

> Let Sweelinck's image attract your eyes,
> The ears he charmed, while still alive:
> And know that, though he lived and died in Amsterdam,
> It was from Deventer that this great bard came.[2]

Revius, a learned man and a distinguished poet, had spent his youth in Amsterdam before he became minister of the Church of St Lebuinus in Deventer (1614). There can be no doubt about the correctness of his statement, and this is a fortunate circumstance since documents are almost entirely missing. The marriage of the parents, Pieter Swybertszoon and Elsken Jansdochter Sweling,[3] took place in the Deventer Church of St Mary (1558), and Jan was born around the month of May in 1562. We know practically nothing about the father and his ancestors. Pieter Swybertszoon was probably a professional musician, but apart from this he must have plied at least one other trade. It is likely that the family moved to Amsterdam in 1563 or 1564. Pieter's position as organist of the Oude Kerk is established from 1566 onwards, but he was probably already employed in this capacity two years earlier. More is known about the mother's family. Her father, Jan

Zwelink, was town surgeon of Deventer (from 1540). Three of her brothers were goldsmiths, and the descendants of one of them, Gerrit Janszoon, became renowned artists (the grandson, Christiaan Swelinck, constructed the famous monstrance in Cologne Cathedral).

Biographers have wondered why Jan Pieterszoon took the name of his mother, yet there is a plausible explanation. The use of family names was still rare at that time, especially in the lower social strata. Most people were identified by their Christian name coupled with a patronymic and an indication of their trade. Thus our composer was for a long time known simply as: Jan Pieterszoon, organist. However, as his social position rose, he must have felt the need for a true family name, and the logical choice was his mother's. This name, still spelt as Swelingh, appears for the first time on the title-page of the *Chansons* published in 1594. His brother Gerrit, born in 1566, also adopted his mother's surname after becoming a successful painter; he was the teacher of Pieter Lastman, who in turn taught the young Rembrandt. It has been suggested that Jan's painted portrait in the Municipal Museum of The Hague (1606) is by Gerrit.

During the 1560s, however, the brothers' careers lay still far ahead. As their father's salary was no more than 60 guilders, he must have had an additional occupation. Yet the family, which also included two daughters, lived in very modest circumstances. Pieter Swybertszoon died in 1573, and although there are indications that during the last years of his life his financial position had somewhat improved, he left practically no inheritance. So the family's situation was far from promising. Fortunately, help came from outside. The exact details are not known, but in the dedication of his First Book of Psalms (1604) to the burgomasters and aldermen of Amsterdam, Sweelinck alludes to the many benefits he has enjoyed 'from the true fathers of his home town' from the time of his youth. One of these benefits may have been the excellent general education he received from the Oude Kerk's parish priest, Jacob Buyck. Buyck was an erudite man and a fervent defender of the Roman Catholic faith; his brother Joost, elected no fewer than sixteen times as burgomaster, was one of Amsterdam's most powerful governors. If Jacob Buyck claimed a fee for his tutoring, he could certainly not have charged it to the widow. So it is a fair guess that the money came from his brother. But what about the boy's musical education? We can assume that until 1573 he learned from his father, but his training can surely not have been complete by then. Who taught Sweelinck his craft?

This question is the first of three problems that have puzzled all the biographers. The other two concern the year of Sweelinck's appointment as organist and, more important, his personal beliefs. These will be dealt with shortly; first, we must discuss the boy's musical tuition.

Mattheson's assertion that Sweelinck studied with Zarlino in Venice has been discounted for a long time. The only extant document revealing anything concrete about the composer's apprenticeship is a notarial act from 1680 which includes a statement by Jacob van Noordt that 'Jan Pieterss. Swelingh . . . had learnt his craft from the Hon. Jan Willemsz'. Elsewhere in the act we read that this musician, who later adopted the family name of Lossy, had been organist in the town of Haarlem. Despite the more than a hundred years which separate this document from Sweelinck's youth, the statement must be considered trustworthy. Jacob van Noordt, a member of a family of Amsterdam organists, became Dirck Janszoon Sweelinck's successor at the Oude Kerk in 1652. There is no doubt that he had known Dirck very well. Moreover, the relationship of Jan Pieterszoon Sweelinck with the Lossy family is attested by the documented fact that in 1598 Lossy's son, Willem Janszoon, became in turn the composer's pupil. In one detail, however, van Noordt's memory must have failed him: Jan Willemsz. Lossy is not traceable as an organist in Haarlem. Instead, he was leader of the town musicians from 1592 until his death in 1629. The error may be explained by the circumstance that both Lossy's son Willem and his grandson Nicolaes had been organists at the Nieuwe Kerk in Amsterdam. Obviously Jacob von Noordt assumed without further consideration that father Lossy had occupied a similar post in Haarlem.

Jan Willemszoon Lossy came from a fairly rich family of Haarlem brewers, and it is unlikely that music was ever his principal means to a living. He is mentioned first as a countertenor and bass shawm player, and later, as has just been said, as leader of the town musicians; two of his sons also belonged to this body. Nothing more is known about his musical activities. Lossy's teaching of Sweelinck has been questioned, especially by Curtis (who makes the unfounded claim that Jan Pieterszoon may have instead studied with the Haarlem organist Floris van Adrichem).[4] The main arguments underlying the doubt are the following. Lossy was not an organist but 'merely' a singer and shawm player; in both capacities he was probably an amateur. Besides, it seems unlikely that the boy studied in Haarlem at a time when he was still under the tutorship of Jacob Buyck in Amsterdam.

Several counter-arguments can be adduced. Amsterdam and Haarlem being only 15 miles apart, weekly visits to the second town are certainly not ruled out, even if the boy had to travel on foot. Besides, we know that Sweelinck's brother Gerrit also received schooling in Haarlem. The fact that Lossy was technically an amateur reveals nothing about the quality of his musicianship. In Sweelinck's time, many distinguished Italian composers including Gesualdo were also amateurs. As for the Netherlands, Constantijn Huygens, secretary to three Princes of Orange and a diplomat of international standing, wrote music of high quality, whereas Jacobus Vredeman, music teacher at the Latin School at Leeuwarden and professional leader of the Collegium Musicum in that town, betrays a rather poor command of counterpoint in his *Musica miscella* (Franeker, 1602). The objection that Lossy lacked a position as organist is likewise invalid; he may have abstained from aspiring to such an occupation. At any rate it does not prove that he was incapable of playing the organ. And finally, even if we assume that Lossy was quite an undistinguished musician, then his case is far from unique in history. A genius need not be taught by a great master. Schubert and Brahms offer clear examples; the latter even bluntly declared that he had learnt nothing from his teacher Eduard Marxsen. On the basis of all these factors I consider it likely that Sweelinck studied with Lossy in Haarlem. This does not, of course, rule out the possibility that in other respects the composer was self-taught.

The second problem, that of the exact date of Sweelinck's appointment as organist of the Oude Kerk, stems from the lack of archival data. Only from 1581 is his position confirmed by documents. Yet we have a credible testimony from Sweelinck's friend, Dr Cornelis Plemp, a Catholic patrician (1574–1638). Plemp read law at Leyden, Louvain, Ingolstadt, Douai, and finally Orleans, where he took his doctorate. Studying at five universities did not lead to a career, however. Plemp disliked the practice of law and, being a man of independent means, spent most of his life as a scholar and prolific writer of mainly Latin verses, associating with learned people like Lipsius, Grotius, and Heinsius, as well as the poets Hooft and Vondel. In his youth he was already an admirer of Sweelinck, who taught him music and became his friend. The amicable relationship lasted for more than a quarter of a century. Now Plemp states in his *Poëmata* (Antwerp, 1631) that Sweelinck had been an organist in Amsterdam 'for 44 years'. If we exclude the improbable possibility of his employment at another church, this would mean that the composer was appointed at the Oude Kerk even before the 'Alteration', that is, in 1577. The facts, or rather the lack of facts, argue for the correctness of

Plemp's statement. After Pieter Swybertszoon's death his post was taken over by Cornelis Boscoop, the composer of a Dutch Psalter for four to six parts set to the same translation as that of Clemens non Papa's *Souterliedekens*.[5] Boscoop died, however, after a few months, and from 1573 to 1578 none of the existing documents mentions the name of a successor. But it is perhaps not a coincidence that on 15 November 1577 a 'meester Baerrent, organist' was buried in the Oude Kerk. This strengthens the likelihood that Sweelinck's career began in the last-mentioned year.[6] The fact that he was only 15 does not weaken the assumption; in the sixteenth century a well-trained young man of that age was considered capable of filling such a post.

The third problem, that of Sweelinck's faith, is the most interesting but also the most difficult to resolve. Up till 1578 he remained, of course, a Catholic; but what happened after the 'Alteration'? Since he was employed from that time onwards by the Protestant magistracy, it is likely that he dutifully adhered to the Calvinist religion. This is all the more probable as during the 1590s three of his children were baptized in the Oude Kerk. Yet even if Sweelinck became a Protestant, he did not hide his sympathy for his Catholic fellows and the Roman musical heritage. The use of Gregorian chant in the *Cantiones sacrae* (1619; dedicated to Plemp) and the inclusion in this collection of a motet set to the antiphon text 'Regina coeli' show that he never disavowed his past. Catholic sympathies are also found in his family, as witness the following examples. Sweelinck's mother and his brother Gerrit almost certainly remained attached to the old faith; during his mother's burial the church bells rang her out with a 'Regina'. As for the composer's son Dirck, he came into conflict with the elders and deacons of the Oude Kerk in December 1644, because he had intended 'to rock the child' (an old Catholic tradition of singing Christmas carols in church) 'and for this purpose invited many papists'. Dirck's brother Pieter, though himself a Protestant, married a woman from a Catholic family; his sister Elsgen's marriage, too, was mixed, her husband as well as her children being Catholics.

On the other hand, Sweelinck kept up close relations with quite a number of Protestant citizens, and his brilliant setting of the Genevan psalter was a real monument of the Calvinist religion. None of the composer's friends belonged to the more fanatic advocates of the Reformation, however; they seem to have been 'doves' rather than 'hawks'. It is even possible that, through the influence of Plemp, Sweelinck sympathized with the (utopian) ideal of the *pax ecclesiastica*, the reunification of Geneva and Rome. We will never know.

A few weeks before the 'Alteration' the uncompromising Jacob Buyck left the city; he ended his life as a parish priest in Emmerich. The event itself passed off rather smoothly. There was much jeering on the part of the population but practically no violence; the monasteries and convents were left untouched, and only the hated Minorites, local representatives of the Inquisition, were treated rather roughly before they were chased out of town. The young Sweelinck must have been deeply impressed by this 'revolution'. Suddenly his knowledge of liturgical chant was of no use; instead, he had to learn the melodies of the Genevan Psalter. The instructions from his new employer, the magistracy, have not been preserved. If they were similar to those in most other Dutch towns, Sweelinck must have played the organ once or twice a day for one hour; in addition, he was probably responsible for the condition of both the large and the small organ in the church. In one respect his position was different, however. It was neither his duty to play the carillon nor the town's harpsichord (during the magistrates' banquets). Consequently his stipend, 100 guilders a year, was very low. Curiously enough, it was not paid by his actual employer (the town) but by the churchwardens. Obviously the magistracy considered the position of the church strong enough to meet these expenses.

In 1585 Sweelinck's financial situation grew precarious. His mother died in that year, so the young man became the family's breadwinner and guardian (there were still two children under age). Once more a magistrate offered help. It is certainly no coincidence that alongside Sweelinck himself, Jan Verhee acted as an executor of the widow's will. Verhee, who held several high municipal offices including that of *president van de schepenen* (chief judge) cared a good deal about the family and especially its musically gifted member. The fact that Sweelinck's salary was doubled is very probably due to his influence with the burgomasters. Nevertheless, the clouds were still not driven away; in 1587 the organist is listed among the citizens incapable of paying their taxes. From then on, however, his fortunes took a favourable turn. His fame as a performer grew rapidly and the magistrates were disposed to raise his salary to 300 guilders, in the event of his marriage. In addition, he was offered the choice between a further 100 guilders and free accommodation in a house belonging to the town. In 1590 the marriage of Jan Pieterszoon and Claesgen Dircxdochter Puyner from Medemblik was duly registered, and the young couple moved into a commodious house in the Koestraat. Obviously, Sweelinck preferred free accommodation to another increase in his salary, the more so as his father-in-law seems to have been a man in a good position. The documents in question suggest that in this instance, too, the magistrates' offer was in fact the doing of Jan Verhee.

Although, despite the rises, Sweelinck's salary was still relatively modest, by this time he must have derived considerable additional income from his activity as a teacher. Throughout his life he was much sought after in this capacity by amateur and professional musicians alike. As for his daily organ playing, there are several reports that it drew a multitude of music-lovers into church. For foreigners, attendance at Sweelinck's 'concerts' became mandatory. In 1594 Count Philip Louis II of Hanau-Münzenberg listed as the principal attractions of Amsterdam the Artillery House, a live elephant in the Hall of the Archers' Guild, and 'hearing the city's organist'. More explicit is the praise of the Venetian ambassador to England, Giorgio Giustiniano, who paid a short visit to Amsterdam in 1606. On the last day he enjoyed the playing of the organist in the main church ('a great, excellent man'); later that evening a number of magistrates including one burgomaster offered him a banquet 'with music by the same organist'. This is one of the rare occasions on which Sweelinck was persuaded to play during a festive assembly of the town's officials. Foreign musicians came as well to his performances. We know that in 1593 Peter Philips went to Amsterdam 'onely to sie and heare an excellent man of his faculties' who cannot have been anyone but Sweelinck. The journey turned out to be risky, however. On his way back to Antwerp, the Catholic Philips, being accused of the intention to murder the Queen of England, spent some time in the notorious prison of The Hague (where he composed his chromatic *pavana* and *gagliarda dolorosa*) but was eventually released on receipt of the Earl of Essex's written testimony.

Sweelinck was not only a great performer; he also had a wide knowledge of organ-building. The magistrates of various Dutch towns asked his advice in matters of repairs or his opinion on newly built instruments. Nine journeys are documented in this connection: Haarlem (1594), Deventer (1595), Middelburg (1603), Nijmegen (1605), Harderwijk (1608), Rotterdam (1610), Dordrecht (1614), Rhenen (1616), and again Deventer (1616). A visit to Antwerp in 1604 had nothing to do with organ-building; instead, Sweelinck bought there a new harpsichord for the Amsterdam magistracy. As far as we know, this journey was the only one he ever undertook outside the territory of the Republic.

11

During the 1590s the first compositions appeared in print. Out of three volumes of French chansons, published in Antwerp, only the last one has survived. Two collections, one for four and five parts (1592), and one for five parts (1593), mentioned in Georg Draudius's catalogues of 1625 and 1610 respectively, are lost. The third volume, the *Chansons à cinq parties*, containing 18 items by Sweelinck and 4 by Cornelis Verdonck (1594), was published by Pierre Phalèse; this is probably also true of the 1592 and 1593 collections. Biographers have made several erroneous statements about these three works. Misled by a misprint in the dedication—it is dated 1584—Bernard van den Sigtenhorst Meyer considered the 1594 volume a reprint of a lost original edition and consequently discussed its contents as the work of a young man of 22 years. His assumption can be easily refuted: the title-page clearly states that the chansons, both of Sweelinck and Verdonck, were 'nouvellement composées & mises en lumière'. As for the two lost works, it has been suggested by Tollefsen that their contents were identical with that of the 1594 volume.[7] In this case, too, the suggestion is invalidated by the words 'nouvellement composées'. Moreover, it is difficult to accept that works which according to Draudius were still available in 1610 and 1625 had to be reprinted only one or two years after their original publication. And finally, four-part chansons cannot have been reissued as five-part ones. However, if Tollefsen's conjecture proves untenable, this does not mean that Draudius's catalogues are entirely trustworthy. The truth about Sweelinck's first two publications has still to be established.

Two sacred compositions are included in *Cinquante pseaumes de David* (Heidelberg, 1597), a collection edited by Louis Mongart and dedicated to a number of unnamed music-lovers in Amsterdam. These are six- and five-part settings of Psalms 3 and 10 respectively. By this time Sweelinck probably had already in mind the setting of the Genevan Psalter. Book I[8] appeared in 1604, Book II in 1613, and Book III in 1614. All three volumes were published in Amsterdam, although they were printed in Geneva. Only the concluding Book IV was entrusted to a Haarlem printer; it appeared a few weeks after Sweelinck's death (1621). Among his vocal works the Genevan Psalter was certainly the longest lived. As late as 1707 the church deacons of Zuoz in the Swiss Engadine purchased a complete set of the psalms in Amsterdam; subsequently, they had the French texts translated into their own language, the Latin dialect of Rhaeto-Roman (so-called 'Romansch'). The manuscripts in question, which were used in the local church until about 1840, are now in the municipal archives. Apart from the translated texts, they are remarkable because of the antiquated musical notation (lozenge-shaped notes). Evidence of Sweelinck's international fame as a musical psalmist is also found in foreign publications. During his lifetime two anthologies with German texts underlaid were published in Berlin (1616 and 1618). On the title-pages the composer is called a 'universally renowned musician and organist'. Further, a German version of the five-part Psalm 72 (Book I) is included with added continuo in the *Erster Theil geistlicher Concerten und Harmonien*, edited by Ambrosius Profe and published in Breslau (1641).

Two other vocal collections were printed during the last decade of Sweelinck's life, both of which form a striking contrast with the austere setting of the Psalter. In 1612 the Leyden branch of the Antwerp firm of Plantin published the *Rimes françoises et italiennes*, a series of amorous poems set for two and three parts. Seven years later the *Cantiones sacrae quinque vocum* appeared in Antwerp, printed by Pierre Phalèse; these motets included settings of Roman Catholic liturgical texts. Taken as a whole Sweelinck's vocal output reflects the diversity of Dutch musical life. If in theory the Protestant and Catholic beliefs were considered incompatible, in musical practice this religious dichotomy became virtually obliterated. There is evidence that 'heretics' and 'papists' frequently joined to sing Latin motets as well as Genevan psalms. The same is true of the division between the sacred and secular spheres; Sweelinck's light-hearted *Rimes*, for example, include a setting of the Lord's Prayer.

While practically all the vocal works have been transmitted in printed editions, none of the instrumental compositions were published during Sweelinck's lifetime. About 70 keyboard pieces are extant, including a few doubtful attributions. They may be divided into five groups: fantasias, echo fantasias, toccatas, variations on sacred tunes, and variations on secular tunes. Almost all these pieces seem to have been composed after 1600. Only two stylized pavans, parodies based on models of John Dowland and Peter Philips respectively, may date from the 1590s (the second piece was probably written on the occasion of Philips's visit to Amsterdam in 1593). There can be hardly any doubt that only a small portion of the composer's instrumental output has survived; furthermore, several preserved compositions, known exclusively from sources dating from long after Sweelinck's death, exhibit rather defective readings. The sole seventeenth-century publication ('Fantasias for three parts in the eight modes', 1630) could have given us fairly authentic musical texts. Unfortunately no copy of this edition by Samuel Scheidt has yet been discovered.[9]

However, despite the imperfect form in which Sweelinck's instrumental output has been transmitted to us, it is mainly on this body of manuscripts that his eminent reputation in the history of Western music has been founded. During the composer's lifetime his keyboard music was already well known in neighbouring countries. In the Fitzwilliam Virginal Book, for example, Sweelinck is represented by four compositions; apart from a toccata by Giovanni Picchi, these are the only foreign works included in this substantial English manuscript. Other pieces were copied and are preserved in London, Oxford, and Liège. However, the bulk of Sweelinck's extant keyboard work was copied by Germans, either in the original Anglo-Dutch notation or in organ tablature. It is in this connection that we arrive at a subject we have not yet discussed: the important school of German organists and composers that owed its existence to Sweelinck's teaching.

Among the first foreign musicians whose study with Sweelinck has been recorded were Paul Siefert and Jacob Praetorius II, who came from Danzig and Hamburg respectively. Siefert stayed in Amsterdam from 1607 to 1609. After his return he worked as organist first in Königsberg, then in Warsaw, and finally in his home town. In 1643 he became involved in heated polemics with the Italian composer and theorist Marco Scacchi, at that time choirmaster at the Polish court. It is chiefly for this dispute that Siefert is still remembered today. Yet his psalm settings and keyboard works are far from negligible. Jacob Praetorius, son of the Hamburg composer Hieronymus, stayed with Sweelinck around the same time as Siefert. When he married in 1608, the Amsterdam organist offered him a work of his own, a five-part *Canticum nuptiale* which was printed in Hamburg in the same year. Like Sweelinck, Praetorius occupied only one post during his whole life, that of organist at St Peter's Church in Hamburg. His compositions include motets as well as instrumental chorale and Magnificat settings. In addition, he had a great reputation as a teacher; both Matthias Weckmann and Berendt Petri studied with him. Sweelinck's most prominent disciples were Samuel Scheidt from Halle and Heinrich Scheidemann from Hamburg. Scheidt stayed in Amsterdam probably during 1608 and 1609. Scheidemann came later; he studied with Sweelinck for three years (from November 1611 to November 1614). In the latter year the teacher wrote a farewell canon for his pupil on the chant melody of 'Ave maris stella'. As both Scheidt and Scheidemann are well known as outstanding German baroque composers, there is no need to describe their respective careers here.

The list of Sweelinck's disciples includes, further, Gottfried

Scheidt, Melchior Schildt, Andreas Düben, Jonas Zornicht, and Peter Hasse, all of whom subsequently obtained important musical posts in or outside Germany. Gottfried Scheidt studied in Amsterdam from 1611 to 1615. Though living somewhat in the shadow of his famous brother Samuel, he was a much respected musician who held the position of court organist in Altenburg; later he became leader of the ducal chapel. Schildt was Sweelinck's pupil during the years 1609–12. He spent his life as an organist in Wolfenbüttel, Copenhagen, and finally his home town, Hanover. Andreas Düben made his career in Sweden. His apprenticeship with Sweelinck lasted no fewer than six years (1614–20). He then went to Stockholm and eventually became the leader of the court chapel and organist of two churches. Jonas Zornicht, from East Prussia, had already visited the Low Countries and Italy before he studied with Sweelinck (1612–14); subsequently he was appointed Kantor of the Old City of Königsberg. As for Peter Hasse, we do not know the exact date of his sojourn in Holland. It probably fell before 1616, the year when he became organist at St Mary's Church in Lübeck. Hasse, an ancestor of the famous eighteenth-century opera composer, left only a few compositions; however, like Praetorius he was in high repute as a teacher and performer. Apart from these musicians, the names of a few other pupils have been recorded: David Aebel (Lübeck), I. Habben and A. Janssen (both Emden), Matthias Leder (Danzig), Ulrich Cernitz (Dömnitz), and Augustus Brücken (Berlin).

In several cases the student's cost of tuition and living were borne by his native town. This is established in the cases of Paul Siefert and Jonas Zornicht, but it may also be true of other pupils. Augustus Brücken's stay was financed by the Elector of Brandenburg. In this instance we know the exact amount Sweelinck could demand for his teaching: 50 ducats annually, that is, about 200 guilders. Its spending power can be easily inferred from a comparison with the sum Brücken received to meet his cost of living: approximately 186 guilders per annum. No wonder Sweelinck ended his life as a prosperous man.

While some of the pupils came to Amsterdam at a fairly young age (Scheidemann, Brücken, Zornicht), others had already been professionally active before (Scheidt, Siefert). It is therefore likely that Sweelinck's teaching was at a 'post-graduate' level. This is not contradicted by the presence of a primer, the *Rules of Composition*, in the first Complete Edition of his works (1896–1901). Although formerly regarded as an authentic work, nowadays the three mid-seventeenth-century manuscripts—which differ among themselves—

15

are considered to represent at best some basic principles of Sweelinck's teaching. Compared to contemporary or earlier theoretical works, the text offers no new viewpoints. Actually, it leans heavily on Zarlino's writings.

Historically speaking, Sweelinck's Dutch pupils are overshadowed by the Germans. While it is likely that as composers they could hardly compete with people like Scheidt, Scheidemann, or Praetorius, the reason for their implicit inferiority is that none of their keyboard compositions or vocal works have survived. Yet among these disciples there were several who became organists of high repute. In the absence of manuscripts or printed collections, the statement that 'Sweelinck's Dutch pupils included no important creative talents' seems rather rash.[10] It is unlikely that Pieter Alewijnszoon de Vooys, who after having studied with Sweelinck was appointed town organist of The Hague (1604), would have been asked by the Amsterdam magistrates to become his former teacher's successor at the Oude Kerk, had he not been considered a musician of considerable stature (being blind and obviously not wanting to change his position, De Vooys made use of the offer only in order to obtain a rise in salary from his municipal employers, with the result that Dirck Sweelinck became his father's successor). The will of the Delft brewer Cornelis Graswinckel (1652) mentions a tablature in-folio by Pieter de Vooys; this indicates that the latter was a composer of keyboard music.

Sweelinck was a sociable man. He had several friends beyond the Republic's borders: the Antwerp lexicographer Franciscus Sweertius, who called him 'mihi amicissimus'; the composer John Bull, who in 1621 wrote a fantasia on a theme of Sweelinck as a musical epitaph; the Königsberg Kantor Johann Stobäus, for whom the Amsterdam organist composed an eight-part wedding-song; and Peter Philips, who continued to honour his colleague as 'a Phoebus or Apollo'. In Amsterdam Sweelinck associated on an equal footing with local patricians. His pupil and friend Cornelius Plemp has already been mentioned. Another pupil was Christina van Erp, the first wife of Pieter Corneliszoon Hooft, who was the son of a prominent burgomaster, and who became the central figure of a brilliant circle of poets, musicians, and scholars. Being Bailiff of 't Gooi, a region east of Amsterdam, he received his guests in the medieval castle of Muyden. The true *Muyderkring* started only towards the end of the 1620s, but already during the last years of Sweelinck's life, Hooft, himself one of the greatest poets of his time, often invited intellectuals and artists to stay with him and his wife for a few days. Plemp's Latin elegy *In*

Mudam, dating from 1624, describes these meetings, and it is noteworthy that the poet laments the absence of the late 'Suelingius Orpheus'. Plemp used to visit Muyden in the company of Sweelinck.

The Dutch fondness for domestic music-making was not restricted to amateurs. We may be sure that, like many Amsterdam homes, Sweelinck's house in the Koestraat was also a centre of musical activity. Both his sons Dirck and IJsbrandt were expert on the keyboard; they may have played other instruments as well and, like everyone else at that time, practised singing. As for the father, we know that he played the lute, since seven pieces from his hand (psalm settings and dances) have been preserved. In addition, he was the composer (or editor?) of a *Nieu Cytherboeck*, unfortunately lost.[11] Printed in 1602 or 1608, this book testifies to the small distance between different social strata, the cittern being traditionally an instrument for the lower classes.

The Calvinist minister and historian Gulielmus Baudartius offers us a unique glimpse into Sweelinck's home. The following passage has been quoted many times, but since it is the only extant 'human' document, it should not be omitted for this biographical sketch.

This Apollo had the nature of most musicians, as was said by a Latin poet:

> *Omnibus hoc vitium est cantoribus inter amicos,*
> *Ut nunquam inducant animum cantare rogati,*
> *Iniussi nunquam desistant . . .*

In other words, one cannot easily induce excellent *musiciens* to sing or to play, but once brought to that point, they find it difficult to leave off. I remember once, with certain good friends, visiting my good friend Ian Petersz. Swelinck with yet other good friends in the month of May, and he at last begining to play the harpsichord, the same continued till about midnight, playing among other things *Den lustelicken Mey is nu in zijnen tijt*, which he, if memory does not fail me, played in five and twenty different ways, now in this, now in that. When we stood up to take our departure, he bade us but listen to this piece again, then to that piece, not being able to stop, such was the very sweet humour he was in, pleasing us his friends, pleasing also himself.[12]

Sweelinck died on 16 October 1621, lamented by many. Hooft, Vondel, Revius, and Plemp wrote epitaphs for him and he was even commemorated in an untitled *coranto*; this was exceptional, since at that time newspapers contained hardly anything other than commercial reports. An uneventful life had ended, standing in curious contradiction to a world-wide fame.[13] But Sweelinck's music did not die with him. After a discussion of his vocal and instrumental output we will come back to the composer's impact on subsequent generations, travelling as far as the early eighteenth century.

II
SECULAR VOCAL MUSIC

The Chansons

Of Sweelinck's chansons, twenty-one are extant in complete form, all but one dating from the 1590s. Apart from the eighteen pieces included in the 1594 volume, two others appeared in Phalèse's collection *Le Rossignol musical* (1597) and one in the composer's *Rimes* (1612).

For a clear understanding of Sweelinck's chanson style we must take a look at the genre's previous history. In the early sixteenth century there were two different stylistic schools, each belonging to a particular geographical area. Parisian composers wrote their chansons, set to epigrammatic or lyric texts, in a simple transparent texture, clearly underlining the poetic metre. Although the upper voice dominates, the inner parts are independent to a certain extent. Homorhythmic settings are rare but include two of the most famous pieces: Sermisy's 'Tant que vivray' and Janequin's 'Ce moys de may'. The charming simplicity of the Parisian chanson was a stylistic novelty in its time, although it is true that the composers used a technique not dissimilar from that of the late fifteenth century. The relationship with the frottola seems obvious but there is no evidence of a direct Italian influence on the genre.

French chansons written by contemporary Netherlands composers were quite different in style. Rooted in the compositional technique of the late Josquin, the works of Gombert, Clemens non Papa, Créquillon, and others exhibit a preference for through-imitation, as a result of which they give the impression of short motets. Because of the contrapuntal texture, the overlapping of phrase endings and beginnings, and the frequent textual repeats, the poetic metre is musically obliterated; the text is almost treated as prose. Although Netherlands composers made ample use of pre-existent melodic material, they rarely presented it as a cantus firmus. In this respect their technique differed from that of the Germans, who at that time still wrote *Tenorlieder*.

During the century's second half the chanson came under the

18

influence of the Italian madrigal. Actually, many composers cultivated both genres. Nevertheless, the setting of French poetry maintained its stylistic independence and underwent its own development. This is especially true of the Parisian chanson. The impact of the aesthetic principles of the *Pléiade* is felt in the output not only of Lassus, but also of Arcadelt, Goudimel, Claude Le Jeune, and Bertrand. The union of poetry and music promoted by Ronsard and his fellow poets eventually led to the more rigid prescriptions of Baïf's *Académie de poésie et de musique*, which cultivated 'vers mesurés à l'antique'. By 1580 contrapuntal treatment of the voices had virtually disappeared from the Parisian chanson. *Airs de cour*, whether 'mesurés' or not, were written in a predominantly homophonic style.

The Netherlands remained untouched by this development. The chansons of Pevernage, Faignient, Castro, Verdonck, and Cornet are characterized by the traditional imitative entries of the voices and by free polyphony occasionally alternating with chordal writing. Modern features are rarely encountered. Only through the expressive setting of certain text fragments did the northern chanson show some indebtedness to the madrigal. In the historical context its style appears rather antiquated, although contemporaries may not have shared this opinion.

Sweelinck's chansons belong to the last-named type. His contrapuntal style is even carried further than that of other Netherlands composers. In this connection the words 'accommodées tant aux Instruments, comme à la Voix' on the title-page of the 1594 volume are quite appropriate. The pieces can be played as well as sung. This does not imply that Sweelinck treated his texts loosely. His musical prosody is almost impeccable, and the occurrence of madrigalisms attests to his concern with the words. However, the qualities of the poem as a whole are less apparent in the musical setting. Compositional technique conflicts with poetic style.

Out of twenty-one texts, six are by Clément Marot, two by Pierre de Ronsard, two by Olivier de Magny, and one each by Guillaume Guéroult, Mellin de Sainct-Gelais, and Philippe Desportes (the remaining eight poems have been transmitted anonymously). Most of these poets lived in the first half of the sixteenth century and Sweelinck's selection from their epigrams could have been made by a Parisian composer of about 1550. With a few exceptions the texts concern rather superficial praise of female beauty or light-hearted *boutades* of rejected lovers. At their best they offer poetic charm without depth of feeling; at their worst, bloodless clichés in the style of the old *rhétoriqueurs*.

19

An example of 'learned' treatment of indifferent words is found in no. 1, 'Ie sens l'ardeur d'amour nouvelle', set to an anonymous text (Ex. 1). The technique displayed in this fragment could have served the setting of any text, not least that of a motet. Sweelinck's chansons include many similar examples, swarming with canonic entries which, though showing his particularly skilful handling of the musical material, do not bear on the poetic content. Ronsard's 'Plus tu cognois' (no. 10), dealing with a not too serious lament of an unsuccessful lover, is entirely set in an abstract way. The same is true of no. 13, 'Si i'ayme ou non' (Sainct-Gelais), the text of which depicts the opposite attitude, that of a lover who refuses to disclose his feelings. Even in the case of an abstract poetic device, suitable for musical 'translation', Sweelinck refrains from applying it. In 'Tes beaux yeux', one of the two 1597 chansons, the poet Magny begins each line with a subject taken from the verb or object in the previous one:

> Tes beaux yeux causent mon amour,
> Mon amour fait que ie desire,
> Le desir m'ard et nuit et iour,
> L'ardeur me donne un grand martire,
> Le martire fait que i'empire,
> L'empirer me livre la mort:
> Et toy qui ne fais que t'en rire
> Ne me daignes donner confort.

Only in the third and fourth lines do the settings of the words in question ('ard' and 'ardeur') show some affinity, the latter being the inversion of the former. Otherwise the composer ignores the poetic device.

Among the means applied by Sweelinck to vary the imitative treatment of the parts, the following may be noted. Double imitation occurs in no. 2, 'Quand ie voy ma Maistresse' (Marot), the second entry being a freely handled inversion of the first. This opening device is carried further in no. 15, 'La belle que ie sers' (anon.), which starts as a double fugue with two different subjects. The same piece offers an example of another peculiarity cherished by the composer: the augmentation of the subject in the lowest part. 'Face donques qui voudra', no. 16, opens with an ingenious three-part canon, the lowest voice of which presents the subject in twelvefold augmentation. Most chansons include homophonic fragments, obviously inserted for the sake of variety; however, only a few pieces start off in this way, such as no. 7, 'Bouche de coral', set to an epigram addressed to Diane de Poitiers by Marot. Canonic treatment of the low voices followed by the same device applied to the high voices occurs in the second stanza of no. 3, 'Elle est à vous, douce Maistresse' (Magny). This imparts to the texture a particular transparency, characteristic of this beautiful chanson as a whole.

The one text asking for an abstract treatment in Guéroult's 'Susanne, un jour d'amour sollicitée' (no. 8). The famous *Chanson spirituelle* of Didier Lupi Second (1548) became the starting point of some 40 settings of this poem by composers from various countries. Practically all of them, in so far as they used the original French text, based their compositions on Lupi's tenor, retaining its second mode transposed. The most widely known setting was by Lassus, but his version is matched by Sweelinck's. The Amsterdam composer entrusted the cantus firmus to the treble (perhaps because a woman is speaking); the other parts, being derived from it, are treated in the usual imitative way.[1] The technical features of this chanson foreshadow the seventeenth-century chorale prelude as exemplified by Pachelbel. Sweelinck's contrapuntal ingenuity is shown in Ex. 2, which includes an inverted motif (marked here with crosses) borrowed from the cantus firmus.

Ex. 2

Most of the chansons are set to a single stanza. Among the four items which have a *seconde partie* there is one (no. 5, 'Vostre amour est vagabonde', set in the twelfth mode) with identical concluding lines; these are accordingly rendered as a musical refrain. However, the first ending is on G, the second on C. The three other bipartite chansons (nos. 3, 13, and 16) are treated in the same way. While it is true that the composer still adheres to the modal system, these related endings may be interpreted as rudiments of tonality. Whatever can be said about his other compositional procedures, in this respect Sweelinck's style was anything but antiquated.

Such are the purely musical qualities which prevail in most of the works. It would be wrong, however, to ignore the importance of the music's occasional relationship with the words. Not only in the past but also in our time, these have been labelled 'madrigalisms', fashionable devices borrowed from the Italians, which in terms of musical structure are of no importance whatever. Various examples from Sweelinck's chansons show the error of this view.

Madrigalisms range from inaudible devices ('eye-music') to refined symbolic expression. A common property is that all of them refer not to a complete poetic thought but only to a single lexical entity. A madrigalism may contradict the context as, for example, when high notes are set to the words 'non in cielo'. In such a case we may speak of a procedure overstepping the bounds of common sense. In general, however, word-painting makes perfect sense, albeit without clarification or expression of the overall poetic idea. Its function lies on another level: the madrigalism is instructive for the composer's subsequent procedures. This is even true of eye-music, as shown by the following example. In no. 2, 'Quand ie voy ma Maistresse' the second of these lines

> S'ailleurs mon œil s'adresse,
> Ce m'est obscure nuict.

are set in black notation. This is inaudible, but the fact that the blackened notes imply the use of triple time induces the composer to change the musical metre. Moreover, the change is stressed by the close of the previous line simultaneously in all the voices, announcing homorhythmic writing. Thus the passage serves the textural variety within the chanson, the style of which is predominantly imitative.

Another example involving eye-music is the beginning of the *seconde partie* of no. 3 (actually the third stanza). The initial word of the line 'Bref, à vous est la belle face' is sung by the highest voice on a dotted breve, once the shortest of all note values but in Sweelinck's time, the longest. This seems to be a case of unintentional irony, but the simultaneous entry of three other parts with minims followed by a pause really does give the impression of brevity. Here again the madrigalism leads to a specific texture contrasting with the preceding and following passages (Ex. 3).

Word-painting may even imply 'cheating' in regard to the sense of the text. The opening line of no. 14, Ronsard's 'Pourquoy tournez vous voz yeux', is semantically unequivocal. The verb 'tourner' can denote 'avert' as well as 'invert' but in this instance the former meaning

Ex. 3

is beyond question. Nevertheless Sweelinck adopts the second connotation as a pretext for an ingenious treatment of the musical subject: three entries (Ct., T. II, and B.) are mirrored by two others (C. and T. I). This procedure of melodic inversion not only continues for 15 bars, it is also applied to the setting of subsequent lines ('Par me voir' and 'D'un seul regard') right up to the end. Actually, the 'false' madrigalism at the opening of this chanson becomes the determinant of its contrapuntal structure.

Other instances of word-painting have a more restricted function, although in these cases, too, they may affect the composition as a whole. Typical means for enlivening the music are melismas like, for example, those on '. . . *cercher* ce que le coeur point' (no. 13); '*travaux*[2] que i'endure' (no. 3, with descending scales covering sevenths and once even a ninth); 'Vostre amour est *vagabonde*' (opening of no. 5, with inversions in the lower parts) and '. . . que ie me fusse liée dedans voz *lacx*' (no. 5, second stanza; here the last word—'snares'—is depicted by a web of melodic lines with dotted notes). All these fragments are treated with superb contrapuntal skill. Madrigalisms of various kinds are found in no. 16 (a setting for three parts of the words 'Vivrons gaillard sans soucy', gradually ascending from Ct.–T.–B. to C. I–C. II–Ct.); no. 6 (sharpened notes on 'ie suis tant *altéré*' as well as a general pause separating 'a peine ne puis ie' from '*retirer* mon aleine'); and finally in no. 3 (a setting for two parts of 'ces yeux deux astres ensemble' assigned to the highest voices).

Two chansons deal with mockingly anecdotal texts, both by Marot. In the *dizain* 'Au mois de May' (no. 17), the poet reproaches a doctor for the bleeding of his beloved: 'You take the natural warmth from her;

24

she is already quite cool and has made me feel it all too well.' Hereupon the doctor retorts: 'Be silent—you shall be satisfied; I draw out the blood that makes her unyielding, so that she will take much pleasure in love in this month of May, which banishes all afflictions.' No sooner said than done. 'She fell in love indeed, but unfortunately . . . not with me.'

This epigram is set in a manner showing Sweelinck's care for an efficacious musical rendering of the words. The first two lines are sung homophonically by the three highest voices, and similar passages occur in the course of the piece. Particularly effective is the setting of the doctor's blunt rejoinder 'tay toy' for the countertenor, echoed simultaneously by the two sopranos and tenor. At the words 'le sang qui la fait rigoreuse' the rhythm slows down (semibreves and minims instead of crotchets and quavers). However, the setting of the concluding line is a betrayal of our expectations. The *pointe* is spoiled by excessive textual reiterations with overlapping entries detracting from the intelligibility of the text. This, to be sure, is our first thought. One would expect the surprising final twist of the little story to be set homophonically without repetition, so that the words would be perfectly intelligible. In discussing the passage, Sweelinck's biographer Sigtenhorst Meyer spoke of misplaced textual repetition.[3] Yet on second thoughts this reproof is quite unjustified, as it results from an anachronistic interpretation of the social situation in which the work was performed. Had Sweelinck written his music for an audience, as most composers did from the seventeenth century onwards, his procedure could indeed have been censured as being ineffective. But in his time there was no audience; chansons were sung in private circles and the only people involved in the performance, the singers, had no need for a dramatic underlining of the epigram's dénouement.

The second piece, 'Tu as tout seul' (1597), is set to Marot's version of an epigram by Martial. It addresses Jan, a seemingly happy man. 'You have all to yourself, Jan, Jan, Jan, your vineyards and pastures, your heart and your money, two different homes; no one could wish for more. You have all to yourself the rewards of your fortune, you have all to yourself your drink and your food. All things you have to yourself, except one: you don't have your wife to yourself.'

The poem is set in a very skilful way. No overlapping entries obscure the enumeration of Jan's riches, each phrase beginning where the previous one end. However, continuity as well as structural unity are guaranteed, especially by the handling of the opening four-note motif set to the words 'Tu as tout seul'; this pervades the entire piece.

25

Presented in its original form as well as in retrograde form (both also augmented), it serves as a countersubject to the melodic material of each of the consecutive phrases (Ex. 4). In this chanson, too, the *pointe* is reiterated. Yet the setting of the last line will disturb the modern listener less than that of the previously discussed piece, the words in question being sufficiently intelligible.

Ex. 4

Sweelinck's chansons show him already near the height of his creative powers. Among those contemporaries who sang these pieces few will have recognized them for what they really were: a first step towards the summit of his vocal output, the Psalter and the *Cantiones sacrae*.

The Madrigals

In comparison with the chanson genre, which apart from Sweelinck seems to have been cultivated only by the mediocre composer Jacobus Vredeman, the setting of Italian texts was practised more widely during the early years of the Dutch Republic. The same Vredeman included seven *madrigaletti* in his collection *Miscella musica* from 1602, but it was above all the Leyden organist Cornelius Schuyt who contributed to the repertory. His *Primo libro di madrigali à 5* (1600) and *Hymneo overo Madrigali nuptiali et altri amorosi à 6* (1611) together contain 36 items. Schuyt had visited Italy in his youth, but a great number of his texts probably came from Holland; at any rate they were written there. Dealing with the praises of Leyden's patricians as well as local brides and bridegrooms, these poems are of inferior quality (though one, the eulogy 'O Leyda gratiosa', is quite charming, and this is also true of the music). The composer's *Hollandsche Madrigalen* (1603) are only incompletely extant and cannot be restored. Generally, their Dutch texts are likewise of low quality. But Schuyt also set poems of high literary value. His two books of Italian madrigals include eight *canzoni* by Tasso, another one by Guarini, and a *sestina* by Petrarch. Living more or less in the shadow of his famous Amsterdam colleague,

Schuyt has been undervalued as a composer. He was an excellent craftsman, however, and his madrigals attain the high average level of his time, Italy included. The same is true of the Delft organist Cornelis Schoonhoven; only one piece of his, included in the 1606 collection *Nervi d'Orfeo*, has survived.

Sweelinck must have been well acquainted not only with these works but also with those of Italian contemporaries. His familiarity with several collections issued in Antwerp by Phalèse (*Ghirlandi di madrigali*, 1601; *Novi frutti musicali*, 1610) may be taken for granted, since they include his own pieces. Moreover, in his *Rimes* he parodied five madrigals from *Harmonia celeste* and *Musica divina*, both dating from 1583 and reprinted many times. Finally, we may assume that Sweelinck knew the book of six-part madrigals by the Dutch émigré composer Joannes Tollius (1597), who sent this work from Padua to Amsterdam with a dedication to the local Collegium Musicum.

Only four of Sweelinck's madrigals have been preserved, two of them incompletely. Because of its missing soprano partbook, 'Hor che soave l'auri'n ogni canto' (à 4) must be considered lost. The six-part 'Chi vuol veder' lacks the quinto; however, this part has been skilfully reconstructed by Max Seiffert in the ninth volume of the first complete edition, and in doing so, he has restored and preserved a masterpiece. The very small number of extant compositions representing a genre which enjoyed a certain popularity in the Netherlands leads to the supposition that Sweelinck must have written many more madrigals. The same may be assumed with regard to Schoonhoven; his six-part 'Nel tempo che ritorna' is of such a high quality that it can hardly have been an *opus unicum*.

Despite Sweelinck's familiarity with the new trends in Italian madrigal writing, he refrained from applying modern devices; this is true also of his Dutch contemporaries. Adherence to the old contrapuntal procedures, as shown in the chansons, appears likewise in the settings of Italian texts. Yet Sigtenhorst Meyer's assertion that in the Northern Netherlands there was no stylistic difference among the genres of madrigal, chanson, and motet is an oversimplification.[4] The discussion of the extant works will show that the compositional technique employed in Sweelinck's madrigals really did possess its own characteristics.

'Madonna, con quest' occhi', for six parts (1601), is set to an anonymous text which seems to be a truncated stanza of a canzone. Two *piedi* of two lines each have paired rhymes but are not followed by the customary *sirima*:

Madonna, con quest' occhi m'hai ucciso;
Quando li miro son saette e foco.

Voltate un poco per donarm'aita;
Tu sei la morte mia, tu sei la vita.

The opening words are set with a canonically treated subject for the second soprano and countertenor. However, because of the absence of rhythmic contrasts, the music gives the impression of quiet homophony. The setting of the second line shows a procedure which is only rarely encountered in the chanson though quite often in the madrigal: the imitative treatment of motifs set to small groups of words by paired as well as single voices. In the present case we have the setting of 'Quando li miro', which stresses the dactylic rhythm and forms a mild contrast with the preceding passage. The words 'saette e foco' lead to an irregular cadence (on A in the seventh mode); however, being overlapped by a new entry ('Voltate un poco'), this may be considered a *cadenza per transito* which does not really overstep the rules. In the compact setting of the poem's second half, the imitative entries are more or less obscured by the equal rhythm pervading the whole piece. The composer makes no attempt to oppose musically the words 'morte' and 'vita'. This madrigal is an intimate little work which interprets its text without any expression of passion.

The anonymous poem 'Poi che voi non volete', set for five parts (1610), is a *madrigale*, the most freely treated of Italian poetic forms. Its five lines include four *endecasillabi* and one *settenario*:

Poi che voi non volete ch'io vi baci,
Occhi prigion d'amore,
Lasciate ch'in voi baci lo mio core,
Che non si disconvien, che per mia aita
Io bac'in voi che può tenirm'in vita.

The insertion of a 'verso rotto' in a group of four 'versi interi' enlivens the metrical structure; the music, too, is more varied than that of the previously discussed piece. Sweelinck's treatment of the opening line seems to confirm the absence of any difference between madrigal and chanson. The successive entries alternating the subject with its inversion remind us of the setting of Ronsard's 'Pourquoy tournez vous voz yeux' (Ex. 5). Cornelis Schuyt, too, employed this device for the opening of his madrigal 'L'anima del cor' (*Hymneo*, no. 17); however, his subject is much more simple than that of Sweelinck. The lively rhythm of the subsequent phrases is partly of purely musical origin, partly an illustration of the final word 'vita', the melismatic

treatment of which was a topos in Sweelinck's time. As in 'Madonna, con quest'occhi' the setting is compact, but a rather long homophonic passage on 'Che non si disconvien' offers a welcome contrast between the upper voices and the whole ensemble.

Both madrigals are pleasant works, but they pale before the setting of Petrarch's sonnet from the *Canzoniere*, 'Chi vuol veder'. Here genius meets genius. The deeply felt words read:

> Chi vuol veder quantunque può natura
> E'il ciel tra noi, venga a mirar costei,
> Ch'è sola un Sol non pur a gl'occhi miei,
> Ma'l mondo cieco, che vertù non cura.
>
> E venga tosto: perche Morte fura
> Prima i migliori, e lascia star i rei:
> Questa, aspettata al regno degli Dei,
> Cosa bella mortal passa e non dura.
>
> Vedrà, s'arriv'a tempo, ogni virtute,
> Ogni bellezza, ogni real costume
> Giunt'in un corpo con mirabil tempre.
>
> All'hor dira che mie rime son mute,
> L'ingegno offeso dal soverchio lume;
> Ma se più tarda havra da pianger sempre.

In free translation:

> Who wants to see what nature and heaven can perform
> among us, let him come and feast his eyes upon her
> who alone is a Sun, not merely in my view
> but in that of the blind world, indifferent to virtue.
>
> And may he come soon, because Death steals
> first the best, leaving the wicked alone:
> This being, awaited at the Kingdom of the Gods,
> a mortal beauty, passes and does not endure.
>
> If he arrives in time, he'll see all that is virtuous,
> all that is beautiful, all regal demeanour,
> united in one body with admirable complexion.
>
> Then he will say that my rhymes are mute,
> my intellect paralyzed by the overwhelming light.
> But if he delays any longer, he will weep forever.

The compositional technique—imitation of motifs, alternation of polyphonic and homophonic passages—does not differ from that of the previously discussed pieces. The essential difference lies in the music's subordination to the words. The inner opposition in the poet's thought, supreme beauty against inescapable transcience, is reflected in the musical texture, which changes more frequently than usual. The composer achieves other contrasts by opposing admonishment and warning ('E venga tosto'—'Ma se più tarda') through homophonic settings to the lively polyphonic celebration of Laura's beauty and virtue. Similar effects are obtained through the antithesis between the 'migliori' and the 'rei', as well as between the sighted poet and the blind world. The latter concept is not only depicted by black notation implying triplets but also by the counterposing of the full ensemble to the three upper voices (Ex. 6). This example of word-painting is one of the many occurring in the piece and showing how madrigalisms can be raised to the level of musical symbolism. They include octave leaps ('ciel', 'Sol', 'costei'); triple time suggesting speed ('E venga *tosto*'); melodic and harmonic rigidity ('e lascia *star* i rei'); application of the rhetorical figure of *anabasis* expressed by ascending scales ('Questa aspettata al regno degli Dei'); once again octave leaps ('Cosa *bella* mortal'), and a high setting for 'ogni *bellezza*'. There are also examples of lively melismas ('ogni real *costume*'); chordal density ('Giunt'in *un corpo*'); textural thinning of the full ensemble to a low-pitched two-part ending followed by an *aposiopesis*, that is, a general pause ('che le mie rime son *mute*'); a high melismatic setting for 'soverchio *lume*'; and long note values (semibreves depicting 'Ma se più *tarda*').

Ex. 6

The enumeration of these devices cannot do justice to the real value of Sweelinck's procedures; they might give the misleading impression of gratuitous artifice. The opposite is true; they disclose the essence of the poetic thought and show the interrelation of various concepts. This is exemplified by the passage quoted in Ex. 7. Heaven, Sun, and Laura ('costei') are united here by a common device, the upward leap of an octave. In addition, wherever possible, the composer depicts the same words by ascending fifths. The fact that 'Sol' first occurs on the note G in the second soprano and at the end of the passage in the bass is very probably mere coincidence; Sweelinck had no need of a pun for his musical translation of the poetic thought. Rather, the use of the two purest intervals to point to the heights of the universe results in a symbolic trinity (in the first of the two concluding tercets the composer harks back to the octave leap, depicting 'cosa *bella*').

In his musical interpretation of the text Sweelinck does not confine himself to melodic, rhythmic, and textural devices. The modal system is also involved in his procedures. The principal mode of the piece, the seventh, is for the first time affected by the surprising use of the triad on B flat at the mention of 'Morte' in the second quatrain. Further on, the same note occurs again with 'mortal', this time embedded in a chord of G, as well as with the words 'passa' and 'non dura'. This results in modal ambiguity. Although there is no question of a real shift to the first mode (*commixtio modorum*), the final D major chord of the *prima parte* can be interpreted as belonging to two different modes, the note D being the *repercussa* of the seventh as well as the *finalis* of the first mode. Towards the end of the sonnet's sestet (*seconda parte*) the B flat returns, conspicuously coupled with the word 'pianger', and persists until the penultimate bar. Broadly speaking, one could say that the seventh mode underlines the positive, the allusions to the first the negative thoughts.

Sweelinck's finesses in setting this poem can only be detected by the analyst or the performer. They will escape the listener, however perceptive he may be. Here again, we are reminded of the music's social function: the work was written for the singers, not for an audience. This implies that it will never become popular in our time. Nevertheless, it is a true masterpiece set to sublime poetry and may justly be considered the peak of the composer's secular vocal music.

The Rimes

The collection *Rimes françoises et italiennes* (1612) consists of twenty-six

items, eleven of which are set for two parts (six French and five Italian texts), and fifteen for three parts (five French and ten Italian texts). In addition, the volume contains a three-part setting of the Lord's Prayer in the rhymed translation by Marot, and a separate four-part chanson ('Rozette'). Apart from an anonymous eight-line poem, all the secular French texts are by Philippe Desportes (1546–1606). These are sonnets from his cycles *Amours de Diane* and *Cléonice*, and a 'Villanelle' from his *Bergeries*. Desportes, the most fashionable French poet during the last decades of the sixteenth century, adhered to the movement of 'pétrarquisme' and cultivated the sonnet with a special care for elegance and clarity of expression. His poetry, however, was rather superficial. Of the Italian texts, until recently only two authors had been identified: no. 10, 'Che giova posseder cittadi e regni', is set to a stanza by Pietro Bembo dating from 1547; no. 8, the ballata 'Io mi son giovinetta', comes from Boccaccio's *Decameron* (Ninth day; tenth novella). To these poets two names can now be added. The words of no. 7, 'Liquide perle Amor', are by Lelio Pasqualino, a canon at the church of Santa Maria Maggiore in Rome, who patronized musicians (including Marenzio) and whose house was a centre of 'virtuosi'. The *Madrigali a cinque voci* by Giovanni Maria Nanino and Annibal Stabile (Venice, 1581) are dedicated to him. 'Qual vive Salamandra', no. 22, is based on a sonnet by Giusto de' Conti, transformed into a *madrigaletto* by an anonymous author.[5] The use of the salamander as a metaphor for an ardent lover is fairly common in sixteenth-century poetry.

On the basis of the two languages one could speak of a mixed collection of chansons and madrigals. Yet conspicuously these genres are not mentioned on the title-page. Moreover, the compositional technique displayed in the settings of both the French and the Italian texts is very much the same. It therefore seems more appropriate to consider Sweelinck's *Rimes* as examples of the *bicinium* and the *tricinium*. While it is true that the textless pieces indicated by these names were mostly written for purely pedagogical purposes—especially in Protestant Germany—the sixteenth-century repertory includes quite a few settings of poetry. Michael Praetorius referred to Monteverdi's *Scherzi musicali* as 'tricinia jocosa'. Sweelinck regarded the *Rimes* as a technical challenge. In the dedication to his friend Jean Ludovicq Calandrini (an Amsterdam merchant), he relates that he 'gave himself up to setting diverting rhymes for two and three parts in order to practice [this kind of composition]'. These words may conform to the obligatory modesty found in so many dedications of the time, yet the composer must have felt the need to adopt a severely restricted scoring as a counterpart to his very elaborate psalm settings dating from the same years.

In the two-part pieces Sweelinck abandoned modern metre and returned to the mensural interpretation of time signatures. As there is no question of musical metre in today's sense of the word, the semicircle at the beginning of each piece should be read as *tempus imperfectum*. The rudimentary tonal harmony, previously used in various chansons and madrigals, is also absent; cadences are mostly *clausulae semiperfectae*, that is, sixths resolving into octaves. The scoring for treble and countertenor or tenor allows frequent crossing of the parts, both of which have a range of an eleventh or a twelfth. Adherence to the principles of the modal system is stricter than in the five- and six-part compositions dating from the previous decades; however, the composer hardly observes the distinction between prescribed and irregular cadences. Chromaticism is only rarely employed, and short deviations from the principal mode are nearly always textually justified.

Several means which Sweelinck used to enhance variety within his chansons and madrigals, such as homorhythmic chordal passages following an imitative treatment of the voices, or the division of the full ensemble into two half-choirs, cannot possibly be applied in a bicinium. The composer compensates for this by the sudden retardation or acceleration of the melodic rhythm. This device, occurring in practically all the pieces, is employed either on purely musical grounds or in illustration of the text. An example of the latter procedure is found in no. 11, 'Garulla rondinella'. The slow rhythm used for the words 'le mie pene' (my grief), contrasts with both the preceding and following passages, which depict the swallow's chirping (Ex. 8). Another means of obtaining variety is the alternation of syllabic and melismatic settings. Long melismas, often textually justified, occur more frequently in the bicinia than in the large-scale works.

Canonic treatment of the voices, both *per motu recto* and *per motu contrario*, is abundantly present in all the two-part pieces.'Ie pars, non point de vous', no. 2, sounds like an excercise in canonic writing. Despite a few madrigalisms this composition shows hardly any affinity with the text and the same is true of no. 1, 'Las! que me sert quand la douleur me blesse', which has the appearance of a study in the application of the Phrygian mode. Elsewhere, too, Sweelinck sometimes seems absorbed by an abstract musical construction. In the *seconde partie* of no. 3, 'Lors que le trait par voz yeux décoché', the text, '. . . est un miroir de voz perfections', calls for a canon by inversion;

Ex. 8

however, the composer renders these words with a literal canon at the
upper octave. On the other hand, several pieces evince a strong
concern for the just expression of the text. This is especially true of the
setting of French sonnets. 'Marchans qui traversez tout le rivage
More', no. 6, is one of Desportes's happy inspirations; it is also the
most attractive among the two-part *rimes*.

> Marchans qui traversez tout le rivage More,
> Du froid Septentrion, et qui sans reposer
> A cent mille dangers vous allez exposer,
> Pour un gain incertain qui voz esprits devore,
>
> Venez seulement voir la beauté que i'adore,
> Et l'objet dont ie sens ma ieunesse embraser,
> Et ie suis seur qu'apres vous ne pourrez priser
> Le plus riche thresor dont l'Affrique se dore.

Voyez les filets d'or de ce chef blondissant,
L'esclat de ces rubis, ce coral rougissant,
Ce crystal, cest ebene, et ces graces divines,

Cest argent, cest yvoyre, & ne vous contentez
Qu'on ne vous monstre encor mille autres raritez,
Mille beaux diamans, et mille perles fines.

The canonic melismas set to the word 'traversez' alternate with the triplets resulting from the black notation ('le rivage *More*'). From '. . . et qui sans reposer' till the end of the sonnet's octave the setting is a continuous chain of canons whose subjects are answered literally or by inversion. The *second partie*, comprising the two tercets, is written in the same vein. Towards the end a long melisma on 'mille autres raritez' is opposed to a *parlando* setting of 'Mille beaux diamans, et mille perles fines' (Ex. 9). Neither the learned setting of these charming lines nor the many examples of word-painting detract from the efficacious declamation of the text. In fact, the piece gives the impression of a spontaneous inspiration.

Sweelinck succeeded almost as well with 'Voicy du gay Printems' (no. 5), which includes opposing images of spring and winter (the latter being set with a touch of the Dorian mode within the principal Ionian), and opposing images of 'l'Amour' and Mars, who is depicted by military triadic motifs. It hardly seems a coincidence that in this case, too, the poem is one of the best in the volume.

In the Italian pieces one finds fewer examples of word-painting. However, a rather abstract text like Bembo's 'Che giova posseder' (no. 10, a *vanitas* poem) affords the opportunity to depict 'esser cantato' by a long melisma, and 'polo' by the highest note of the modal scale. In addition, the attractive setting of 'Garulla rondinella' (see Ex. 8 above) is quite dependent on the text, albeit without madrigalisms proper. One Italian poem, 'Morir non puo' (no. 9), is a dialogue, the first stanza being spoken by the lover and followed by the lady's *riposta*. Although from a musical point of view the piece is of high quality, as a dialogue it proves a failure. The text, dealing with the rather artificial problem of whether a heart given away is capable of dying, cannot be rendered by a bicinium; it compellingly calls for solo voices. In this respect, a comparison with the witty and dramatically arresting 'Serenata' and 'Riposta dalla finestra' from Constantijn Huygens's monodic *Pathodia* (1647) is most instructive.

The tricinia present greater variety of compositional procedure than the bicinia. The lowest voice, though usually a tenor, is occasionally treated as a harmonic bass with leaps of fourths and fifths. This

Ex. 9

happens in homophonic passages which tend towards 'tonal' writing. Elsewhere, one of the parts is opposed to the two others, which proceed in thirds or sixths. However, the main characteristics of the bicinia are also found here. Voices cross frequently, the tenor sometimes rising above the countertenor as high as a tenth (for example in the setting of the first quatrain of no. 12, 'Ie voy mille clairtez'). Although there is less canonic writing, free imitation is found in all the pieces. Frequent rhythmical contrasts between consecutive passages, resulting from the interpretation of the text, also remind us of the two-part *rimes*. In general, however, the tricinia draw nearer to the chanson and the madrigal than do the bicinia. For instance, in no. 17, 'Facciam, cara mia File', Sweelinck employs a device often encountered in the chansons of 1594 and 1597: an imitatively treated subject presented in fourfold augmentation by the lowest voice. As in the two-part works, the French texts afford more opportunity for madrigalisms than the Italian, yet the latter include some lines which call for pictorial treatment. Hence the setting of 'guarda non *imitare*' is (ironically) imitative; the same device is applied so the words '. . . de colombe *impara* amare' and 'Da loro i modi *impara*' (see no. 16, 'Lascia Filli'). The rhetorical figure of *katabasis* (a descending scale) combined with a traditional symbolic procedure, *fauxbourdon* (denoting sadness), occurs in no. 14, 'Un iour l'aveugle Amour'. The text speaks for itself (Ex. 10). In no. 15, 'Mon Dieu, que i'ayme ma Déesse', a motif originating from the word-painting recurs later in a freely inverted form. The obvious implication is that 'laughing' ('ris') is the main characteristic of the lady's 'charm' (Ex. 11). The same piece includes a rare example of white notation; *note bianche* set to the words 'sa blanche main' are preceded and followed by *note nere*.

As in the bicinia, one of Desportes's best poems gives rise to the most attractive music. The text of no. 13, 'Yeux qui guidez mon ame', is very 'pétrarquiste' (though comparison with Petrarch's sonnets would prove devastating for the French poet). Sweelinck's setting is full of melodic garlands, sung simultaneously by two or even three voices and alternating with other textures. Particularly impressive are the imitatively treated ascending scales set to the words 'C'est vous qui

Ex. 10

Ex. 11

40

me'enseignez le beau chemin des cieux'. But the composer did not always need a text of high quality to produce charming music. The Italian verses, five of which deal with 'kisses' (a fashionable subject in light sixteenth-century poetry, derived from Horace, Ovid, Catullus, and other classical writers), hardly possess any literary merit. Yet pieces like 'Lascia Filli' (no. 16), 'Facciam, cara mia File' (no. 17), and 'Dolci labri amorosi' (no. 21), belong to the most attractive of the volume.

Five compositions, not discussed above, make use of pre-existent material. These are parodies of two madrigals by Luca Marenzio, and one each by Domenico Ferrabosco, Andrea Gabrieli, and Giovanni de Macque. As has been said before, Sweelinck became familiar with them through the reprints in collections issued by Phalèse. Several of these pieces belonged to the most famous in the sixteenth-century repertory. Marenzio's 'Liquide perle Amor' is the first item of his *opus primum*, Madrigals for Five Voices, 1580. Its fame was so great that it was even mentioned in another madrigal text, 'Donna, se quel ohimè', set by Benedetto Pallavicino, who also quotes the music (*Quinto libro a cinque voci*, 1593). Carlo Milanuzzi included a Mass on 'Liquide perle Amor' in his *Armonia sacra* (1622), and as late as 1640, Pietro della Valle speaks of the popularity of Marenzio's piece (*Della musica dell'età nostra*). The four-part setting of Boccaccio's 'Io mi son giovinetta' by Ferrabosco, first published in a collection dating from 1542, was likewise very famous. It served as a model for two of Palestrina's Masses, one for four and one for six voices. Gabrieli's 'Dolcissimo ben mio' is from his second book of six-part madrigals (1580). The composer himself transformed this work into a motet ('In tribulatione'); in addition, there is a version set to Italian spiritual verses as well as a transcription for lute.

Sweelinck's parody technique, including reduction of four or five parts to two, and six parts to three, raises interesting points. The task of transforming the five-part 'Liquide perle Amor' into a bicinium (no. 7) would seem a *tour de force*. The composer succeeded by using Marenzio's material in a special way and adapting it to a linear two-part texture. Instead of presenting the opening motif on D and reaching the treble's highest note G in the very first bar, Sweelinck begins on the lower fifth and achieves the climax more gradually through a repeat of the motif, arriving at the high note only in bar 2 (Ex. 12). Subsequently, the motif set to the second half of the opening line ('. . . da gl'occhi sparse') is first presented in the imitative manner employed by the Italian composer (the second entry after one

Ex. 12

(a) Marenzio

Li - qui-de per - le A - mor da gl'oc - chi spar - se,

Li - qui-de per - le A - mor da gl'oc - chi

Li - qui-de per-(le)

Li - qui-de per - le A - mor

(b) Sweelinck

Li - qui-de per - le A - mor, li - qui-de per - le A - mor

Li - qui-de per - le A - mor da gl'oc - chi

semibreve) and then as a stretto (at the distance of a minim). The latter procedure, which results in a heightened tension, is entirely Sweelinck's. Other deviations from the original setting include an ascending leap of a minor sixth on the words '. . . ma lass' ohimè', which intensifies their emotional force, and a canon at the upper fifth on 'Ahi, che bastava solo/A darmi morte'; this subject, too, subsequently appears in stretto. Finally a second repeat presents the canon at the unusual interval of a seventh.

In accordance with early madrigal style, Ferrabosco's setting of 'Io mi son giovinetta' is mainly homophonic. Sweelinck transforms the piece into a true linear bicinium (no. 8). His opening phrase employs material from the pre-existent treble and bas parts. This material is later exchanged by the two voices (Ex. 13).

Similar transformational procedures are employed in the three-part parodies. 'Dolcissimo ben mio' (no. 24) first presents a pared-down version of Gabrieli's opening phrase but then follows it with an imitative passage set to the second line, 'Speme di questo core'. The subject, with its upward leap of a fourth, is borrowed from the original bass part. Subsequently, the occurrence of a downward leap of the

42

same interval in the setting of 'In premio del mio amore' enables the Amsterdam master to construct another imitative passage, which is virtually the inversion of the first.

Many more examples of the composer's ingenious transformational procedures could be given, but detailed analyses would exceed the scope of this study. The reader is referred to the original madrigals, four of which are available in modern editions.[6] He will discover that, far from being mere arrangements, Sweelinck's parodies are valid compositions in their own right.

Little needs to be said about the concluding chanson, the four-part 'Rozette' (no. 28). The work clearly shows the development of the composer's style since the publication of his first volume, eighteen years earlier. The texture has gained in transparency and equilibrium; Sweelinck has achieved a just balance between simple homophonic

Ex. 13

settings (often featuring the alternation of paired voices) and the application of contrapuntal devices. In this way the music does justice to the light-hearted text on the traditional theme of the flighty young shepherdess. A refrain common to all four stanzas also functions musically as a means of unification. It is characteristic of Sweelinck's care for structural balance that in stanzas 1 and 3 this refrain ends on the fifth degree of the scale, in stanzas 2 and 4 on the *finalis*.

A final word about performance practice: Seiffert, van den Borren, and Sigtenhorst Meyer all pleaded for a harmonic support by a keyboard instrument, especially with regard to the bicinia. Today it seems hardly necessary to provide arguments for the rejection of this proposal. However difficult it may prove to maintain the right pitch in the performance of the two-part *rimes*, they ought to be sung by solo voices alone without any reinforcement or addition. As for the tricinia, doubling of the separate parts is not absolutely unacceptable, although in this case, too, solo voices are preferable. The same is true of performance by instruments. Sweelinck's subtle interpretation of the text in these delightful miniatures is too precious to be sacrificed.

Nuptial Songs and Canons

During the late sixteenth and early seventeenth centuries, the practice of writing nuptial songs was widespread in Germany. In Holland, too, this genre was cultivated, as many works by Cornelis Schuyt attest. Among his Italian and Dutch madrigals there are no fewer than fourteen items composed for specified or unspecified weddings. Sweelinck left three nuptial songs which, unlike those of Schuyt, are set to Latin texts and may therefore be considered secular motets. It is characteristic of the composer's cordial relationship with his pupils that one of them is written for the wedding of Jacob Praetorius, who in 1608 married Margarita a Campis (her name is spelt thus on the title-page of the edition published in Hamburg; she may have been a Dutch girl, Margaretha van Kampen). This work, set for five voices to an undistinguished occasional text, is in two parts, the first addressing the bridegroom, the second the bride. The fact that the opening phrase reappears in strict inversion at the beginning of the *secunda pars* has a clear symbolic meaning: let husband and wife be each other's mirror. These opening passages are written canonically for the upper and middle voices, the bass acting as a *fondamento* in very slow rhythm. Contrapuntal treatments also occur on the words 'sorte beato' and 'Nympharum decus albiarum'; in the second case the subject is answered by inversion. Elsewhere, the texture is more or less homophonic.

A second nuptial song, *Melos*, has come down only with Latin paraphrasing words by Johannes Stobaeus, who published the work in 1638. Although there is not the slightest evidence that this distinguished Königsberg Kantor ever visited Holland, it seems that he and Sweelinck were on friendly terms. The Amsterdam master wrote another *Canticum nuptiale* for Stobaeus' third marriage, with Regina Möller. This work, set for eight voices, was also printed in Königsberg (1617). Since the text is that of Psalm 17 (after the numbering of the Vulgate), it shall be discussed in the next chapter. In the case of *Melos*, we do not know the original words or even the language used. In terms of abstract music, it seems an attractive piece with felicitous contrasts between homophonic and contrapuntal passages. The style is more or less that of Sweelinck's madrigals.

Of the numerous independent canons the composer must have written during his life, only seven are extant. They include settings of biblical and liturgical texts (for example, 'Vanitas vanitatum et omnia vanitas' and 'Beatus qui soli Deo confidit et laborat'), as well as a proverb ('Sine Cerere et Baccho friget Venus'). Serving as pieces to enlarge collections such as the famous 'Livre septiesme', or as contributions to *alba amicorum*, their importance is mainly due to the fact that they include four autographs, the only such manuscripts that have come down to us. Yet one of them is of both historical and musical interest. This is a piece based on the liturgical melody of the hymn 'Ave maris stella'. Sweelinck wrote it as a farewell gift for his pupil, 'the honest young man, Henderick Scheijtman [that is, Scheidemann] of Hamburg'. The textless liturgical tune is presented as a cantus firmus around which two canonic voices, which end in a hocket-like fashion, entwine themselves. Here we have another example of the composer's benign attitude towards his students.

III
SACRED VOCAL MUSIC

The Psalter

Sweelinck's setting of the Genevan Psalter marks the end of a development which began in the 1540s. Before I present a general view of this polyphonic repertory, a few words must be said about the pre-existent material: the texts and the tunes. Curiously enough, the metrical and rhymed psalm translations used by the Calvinists originated in a Catholic sphere: the French court. In 1537 Clément Marot offered his 30 psalms to King Francis I. Sung to popular melodies, they became the fashion of the day; they even found favour with Francis's arch-enemy, the Emperor Charles V. The collection was printed, however, by Protestants. During his exile in Strasburg Calvin attended to its publication. After his return to Geneva in 1541, where in the following year he was joined by the poet, nineteen more psalms appeared in print, together with a number of canticles. Marot died in 1544 and the remainder of the Psalter was subsequently translated by Théodore de Bèze. This author, a theologian and a humanist rather than a true poet, wrote in a style quite different from that of his predecessor. Because of this he has often been criticized (even in his own time Guillaume Guéroult compared Marot to Amphion and de Bèze to Midas). The complete Genevan Psalter appeared in 1562.

A number of the melodies were borrowed by Calvin, during his exile, from local songbooks and from compositions by the Strasburg Kantor Matthias Greiter. In Geneva the singing master and musical theorist Loys Bourgeois composed, arranged, or left untouched 85 tunes: after his departure from the city in 1552 the remaining melodies were supplied by a Maistre Pierre (his identity is uncertain, as there were at least four musicians of that Christian name in Geneva). The Psalter proper contains in total 124 tunes, 20 of which serve for more than one psalm. Although rhythmically altered and metrically regularized, this musical corpus is still used today in most Calvinist churches.

The origin of the melodies, in so far as they were not freely

46

composed, has been for a long time a matter of dispute. The fact that the first half of the tune of Psalm 72 is practically identical with the tenor of Josquin's 'Petite camusette' led to a supposition that Bourgeois's principal source was the French chanson of his time and of the previous generation. Since the publication of Pidoux's thorough study, however, we know that the connection with Gregorian chant is much stronger.[1]

Polyphonic settings of items from the Genevan Psalter date back even to the time when it was still incomplete. Among the earliest are those by Pierre Certon (1546); they were freely composed, that is, without a cantus firmus. Loys Bourgeois himself set Marot's psalms for four parts homophonically with the tune in the tenor; in addition, he wrote twenty-four settings in a variety of styles including that of the motet. Other composers of polyphonic psalms (inserted invariably in chanson collections) were Janequin (1549), again Certon (1555), Arcadelt, and Ferrier (both 1559). All of them employed the Genevan texts and tunes. It is striking that throughout the century Catholic musicians contributed to the repertory. Even Lassus and Philippe de Monte wrote psalms based on the Huguenot melodies.

Soon after the textual and musical completion of the Psalter several composers undertook the task of setting all 150 psalms. Among them were some minor figures: Sureau and Servin (both 1565), Santerre (1567), and Pascal d'Estocart (1583). But the most prolific and influential musical 'psalmist' was Claude Goudimel. He left three settings of the Genevan Psalter, two of which were complete. His first collection, a set of eight books containing psalm motets (1551–66), remained unfinished. In a different sense, however, these works are complete in that they present settings of all the verses of each psalm (including those of Psalm 119, running to twenty-eight stanzas). In general, the style resembles that of the mid-sixteenth-century motet, the pre-existent melody being divided among the voices and supplied with freely invented countersubjects. The second collection (1564) presents the psalm tune in the tenor (exceptionally, in the treble) against which the other parts are set in note-against-note fashion. This Psalter became so popular, in France as well as in Holland, Switzerland, and Germany, that people believed Goudimel to be the composer not only of the settings but also of the tunes themselves. In the third collection (1568), the cantus firmus, which, as in the second collection, determines the length of each psalm, is assigned to the highest voice; the three other parts derive their melodic material from it, imitating each other.

After Goudimel, who was among the victims of the 1572 massacre in Lyons, Claudin le Jeune became the principal composer of Genevan psalms. His output, which shows him to be scarcely less prolific than his predecessor, includes 347 psalm settings, mostly published after his death (1600). In the *Dodécacorde* (1598), which contains works for two to seven parts in the twelve modes, he displays a particularly brilliant style. Le Jeune's complete Psalter for four and five parts (1601) is much simpler; this opus became almost as popular in Holland as Goudimel's 1564 collection. It is characteristic that the *Dodécacorde* was printed in La Rochelle with a privilege granted by the Dutch Republic's States General. The 1601 Psalter, on the other hand, was reprinted with underlaid Dutch texts in Leyden, Schiedam, and Amsterdam. The pocket format of these editions (12mo) points to their widespread use. Le Jeune was the first composer to set psalms as 'musique mesurée'; 26 such settings appeared in 1606 for two to eight parts (the 'measured' translations are by Baïf and d'Aubigné). This volume was likewise well known in Holland. As late as 1663 the greatest authority in the realm of Calvinist theology, the Utrecht professor Gisbert Voetius, belied his undeserved reputation as an enemy of music by expressing his great admiration for the psalms of Claudin.[2]

The above observations lead us to consider the practice of psalm singing, monophonic as well as polyphonic, in the Low Countries. The earliest metrical Psalter preceding the Genevan one was published by the Antwerp printer, Simon Cock, in 1540. This was the *Souterliedekens*, the texts of which are adapted to the tunes of Dutch folksongs. Although not explicitly Protestant, these psalm translations betray Lutheran influence derived from the Dutch Bible of 1526. The collection's popularity is attested to by the appearance of at least 33 editions up till 1613. Other Psalters by Jan Utenhove (1551–65) and Lucas de Heere (1562) were partially or wholly translated from Marot and de Bèze, and were intended to be sung to the Genevan tunes. Yet they found no acceptance within the Dutch Reformed Church, whose synod preferred the version of Petrus Dathenus (1566). This last Psalter features a painstakingly literal translation from the French; unfortunately, it is of low poetic quality. Dathenus's psalms were used in Dutch churches until 1773.

Because of the immense popularity of psalm singing, which caused people to forsake Mass, the Catholic ecclesiastical and secular authorities had a problem. They could not possibly raise objections to the scriptural words, hence the publication of the untranslated

Genevan Psalter by Plantin in Antwerp (1664) was at first permitted. Later, however, it was condemned on the flimsy grounds that although the texts were sacred, the melodies were heretical. In 1666 there was a short period of permissiveness, but after the arrival of the Duke of Alva with his Spanish army, psalm singing in the vernacular became a capital offence punishable by death.

As for polyphonic settings of Dutch Psalters, only three sixteenth-century collections are extant, all of them based on the *Souterliedekens*; they are by Jacobus Clemens non Papa (à 3; 1556–7), Gherardus Mes (à 4 but with only two partbooks preserved; 1561), and Cornelis Boscoop (à 4, 5, and 6; only 50 four-part psalms were published in 1568). There can be no doubt that Dathenus's Psalter was also set polyphonically more than once (for instance, the *CL Psalmen Davids* for four to eight parts by a certain David Jansz, Amsterdam 1600); none of these works has survived, however. Early settings of Marot's un-translated texts include individual pslams by Appenzeller, Manchicourt, and Waelrant inserted in chanson books. Only one Netherlands publication was entirely devoted to Marot's psalms; the *Pseaumes cinquante* by Jean Louys (Antwerp 1555). This rather obscure composer set the Genevan tunes in a dense, Gombert-like style. More akin to Sweelinck's idiom are the occasional settings of French psalms dating from the late sixteenth century. In his four Genevan psalms, the Catholic Andreas Pevernage employed practically every compositional technique known to his time in order to promote the expression of the text. Other composers from the Southern Netherlands, who based their works on both the Calvinist texts and tunes, include Noë Faignient and Séverin Cornet. In the Dutch Republic itself Sweelinck had no forerunners.[3]

Sweelinck's Psalter contains 153 settings of Genevan psalms (three appear in two different versions). They were published in four voluminous instalments. Book I (1604) runs to 50 items with an additional 'Cantique de Siméon'; 10 of these are for four, 22 for five, 18 for six, and 1 for seven parts. The vast majority (46) set only the first verse of each psalm.[4] Of the twelve verses of Psalm 136 the composer retained the first two; the remaining four texts, including that of the 'Cantique', were set complete. Book II (1613) contains 30 psalms. Here the number of texts set *tout au long* is proportionately augmented, with 8 complete and 4 partial settings against 18 single-verse items. The scoring likewise evinces a shift towards larger dimensions: 6 pieces are for four, 10 for five, 11 for six, 1 for seven, and 2 for eight parts. This tendency culminates in Book III (1614), which also contains 30 psalms; however, the total quantity of music in this book surpasses by far that of each of the previous instalments. No fewer than 15 texts are set complete; several of these comprise six or more stanzas, for instance Psalms 16 and 110. The seven partial settings also include some particularly extended pieces, such as Psalm 103 with seven verses. Unlike those in Book I and II, the 8 single-verse psalms form only a minority. The scoring speaks for itself: 5 psalms are for four, 7 for five, 8 for six, 2 for seven, and 8 for eight voices. Surprisingly, this truly monumental collection concludes with an intimate three-part setting of the Lord's Prayer ('Oraison dominicale'); the same piece had already appeared in the composer's *Rimes*.

It seems as if in Book IV (1621) Sweelinck returned to the less virtuosic style of Book I. More plausible, however, is the assumption that most of its content dates from the first decade of the century. Of its 43 items, 32 are single-verse settings; 7 texts are partially set, and 4 are *tout au long*. The scoring, too, follows approximately the pattern of distribution seen in the first instalment: 8 pieces are written for four, 23 for five, 7 for six, 2 for seven, and 3 for eight parts. As the concluding volume was published a few weeks after Sweelinck's death, we might well question whether it represents a truly completed collection. At all events, Psalm 139 has an unfinished appearance, the first stanza being set for five parts and the second for two. In no other psalm did the composer use a smaller number of voices for the last verse.

Sweelinck employs in his Psalter almost all the techniques and styles of the previous century. Since they often change within a single psalm, a smaller unit should be taken as a starting-point for discussion: the verse. Yet even within the setting of a stanza the composer occasionally shifts from one procedure to another. Therefore any classification can only produce a rough picture. A complex work of art like Sweelinck's Psalter lends itself with great difficulty to a division into strict categories.

Nevertheless, we may distinguish three types of setting: (1) verses with the integral cantus firmus in one of the parts; (2) verses with a freely treated cantus firmus in one or more parts; (3) verses without a cantus firmus. Quantitatively, these groups are not at all equal. Out of a total of 288 verses, 98 belong to the first category. They include 31 verses with the tune in the treble, 10 with it in the countertenor, 47 with it in the tenor, and 9 with it in the bass. In addition, the six-part Psalm 18 (Book IV) presents the cantus firmus during the first four lines in the treble, but during the remaining eight in the tenor. The second group, which contains the freely treated Genevan melody, is almost twice as large, encompassing 185 verses. In contrast, only five verses are set without reference to the prescribed melody. These verses invariably occur in the middle of complex settings whose other stanzas use the cantus firmus either strictly or freely.

Within these groups, especially the first two, we find a great variety of procedures. It is true of course that verses set with an unaltered cantus firmus necessarily limit the composer's freedom. The length of the melody determines that of the setting as a whole, which can only be extended by means of a few introductory bars and a prolongation of the melody's final note. Moreover, the melody itself fetters, to a certain extent, the contrapuntal lines and harmonic progressions of the other parts. Nevertheless, Sweelinck manages to employ a number of different procedures ranging from simple homophonic settings to ingenious contrapuntal textures. The material of the latter is either derived from the cantus firmus or based on a countersubject. Generally, the 'free' parts are set with shortened note values, entailing textual repetitions which enhance the liveliness of the music. A characteristic example is offered by the second verse of Psalm 27 (Book II), bars 11 ff. (Ex. 14). The introductory bars contain either anticipatory imitation of the Genevan tune or a likewise imitatively treated countersubject. In Psalm 36 (Book II), various parts imitate a freely invented opening melody in preparation for the entrance of the cantus firmus; in half of the imitations, the subject appears in inverted form (Ex. 15).

Verses set with a freely treated cantus firmus offer a wider range of procedures and techniques. The given melody is mostly presented in the treble with shortened notes values and always rhythmically altered. Thus it stands no longer in opposition to the other parts. Its continuity is frequently interrupted by freely invented phrases set to textual repetitions. Small melodic deviations within the tune itself are far from exceptional; in those cases, however, the 'correct' notes occur in another part, for preference in the tenor. Nor is the migration of the tune from the treble to one or more of the lower voices a rare occurrence. In principle, the whole ensemble may share scraps of the Genevan melody. Contrapuntal textures are found in practically every psalm. They include the complete array of polyphonic devices: literal imitation, free imitation, inverted imitation (also strictly canonic), augmentation or diminution in one or more parts, and combined imitations, free or canonic, of the tune and a countersubject. A striking

51

Ex. 14

example, taken from Psalm 138 (Book I), bars 26 ff., was included in Sigtenhorst Meyer's book.[5] As it seems the *ne plus ultra* of contrapuntal ingenuity, it may also be shown here. Based on two motifs borrowed from the psalm tune ((*a*) and (*b*)), the fragment additionally contains a free element (*c*). All three are used imitatively in a particularly intricate texture, including the inversion and augmentation of the motifs (Ex. 16).

Example 16 occurs in the coda following the complete setting of the stanza. Such an extension, found in many pieces belonging to the second group, is particularly suited to the display of contrapuntal

Ex. 15

Ex. 16

(a) cantus firmus
(b) cantus firmus
(c) free
Tant es - ti - me - e, et fe - au - té, et fe - au - té,
Tant es-ti-me - - e, et fe - au - té, et fe - au - té, tant
(es)- ti - me - e, tant es - ti - me - - e, et fe - au - té, et
(esti) - me - e, et fe - au - té, et fe - au - té, et fe - au -
tant es - ti - me - e, tant es - ti - me - e, tant es - ti - me -
es - ti - me - - - - - - - - e, tant es - ti -
fe - au - té tant es - ti - me - e, tant es - ti - me - e,
- té tant es - ti - me - e, tant es - ti - me - e, tant
- - - - e, tant es - ti - me - e, et
- me - - - - e, tant es - ti - me - - e,
tant es - ti - me - e, et fe - au -
es - ti - me - e, tant es - ti - me - e, et

proficiency. The opposite technique, simple homophonic setting of the given melody, is also frequently encountered, especially in triple time as well as common time sections of four-part settings. These include the portions for 'half-choir' in psalms set for eight parts, for example, those in Book III (Psalms 41, 42, and 131; also the seven-part Psalm 148) and Book IV (Psalms 18, 76, and 111). Although dividing of the ensemble is quite common in these works, only one is written explicitly for *cori spezzati*. This is Psalm 113 (Book III), the setting of which resembles that of elaborate Venetian psalms sung during Vespers.

The last-named piece includes a stanza (verse 3) which belongs to the five items set entirely without cantus firmus. Another eight-part example from this small group is found in Psalm 111, verse 5 (IV). Here the composer's freedom results in an amazing variety of procedures employed within the limited scope of a single six-line verse. Its first half is set for four parts: a strict canon (line 1) is followed by a free contrapuntal setting (line 2) and the interplay of two pairs of voices, one imitating the other by inversion (line 3). The second half of the stanza begins with a strictly homorhythmic setting of line 4 for five parts; this is literally repeated by another five-part ensemble (line 5), the two countertenors singing in both groups. Only the concluding line is set contrapuntally for all the eight voices, the first bass illustrating the words '. . . qui touiours dure' by means of a longa. Unlike these spectacular eight-part settings, the remaining three verses lacking the Genevan tune are small-scale pieces reminding us of the *Rimes*: Psalm 27, verse 4 (à 3), and Psalm 28, verse 3 (à 2) and verse 4 (à 3), which are included in Book II. Freed from the yoke of the cantus firmus, Sweelinck sets almost every line of these stanzas as a strict or free canon.

So far we have examined the psalm settings in relation to the presence or absence of the pre-existent melody. Another distinction can be made between motet-like and madrigal-like settings. While it is true that the difference is sometimes blurred, many verses clearly conform to one of these two categories. Motet-like textures occur both in pieces with a strict and a free cantus firmus. Examples include Psalm 139, verse 2 (IV) and Psalm 91 (II). The imitative entries, the quietly flowing rhythm and the absence of long passages *a note nere* mark these settings as true psalm motets. Madrigal-like pieces with a freely treated cantus firmus are abundantly present in all four books. They predominate especially in the six- and seven-part psalms. The use of a strict cantus firmus, on the other hand, hardly seems compatible with a madrigalesque style. Examples are nevertheless found among the six-part psalms in Book III, for instance Psalm 4, all four verses of which contain the integral Genevan melody.

In setting his Psalter, Sweelinck found his freedom restricted not only by the pre-existent material but occasionally also by other factors. No fewer than twenty melodies serve for more than one psalm. In these cases the composer felt obliged to set the tune in different, indeed contrasted ways. Psalms 24 (I), 62 (III), 95 (I), and 111 (IV), all of which are based on the same cantus firmus, differ markedly in scoring and compositional technique. Psalm 24 (à 4) presents the unvaried tune first in the treble and then in the tenor. The other parts, imitating the pre-existent melody as well as each other, enliven the setting greatly with their shortened note values. Psalm 62 (à 7) is based on a freely treated cantus firmus and written in a serious madrigal style entailing the occasional division of the ensemble into two homophonic half-choirs. In Psalm 95 (à 6) the tune is also presented freely in the treble and various other parts; however, in accordance with the joyful text the style is much more lively, resembling that of a *madrigaletto*. Finally, Psalm 111 (à 8) is composed *tout au long*. This impressive work exploits all the potentialities of its eight-part scoring.

Compositions sharing not only the pre-existent melody but also the text offer a still strong challenge. We do not know why Sweelinck set Psalms 3, 27, and 134 twice. All three of them had appeared in a single-verse form in Book I; perhaps he or his Amsterdam friends were dissatisfied with this limited selection from the complete texts. Be this as it may, the second settings, which were new in every respect, contain all the stanzas of the psalms in question. They are included in Books II (Psalm 27) and III (Psalm 3 and 134).

Quite another task was the reworking of existing compositions. This is the case with the two psalms which had already appeared in Mongart's collection (1597). They are Psalm 10 (à 5) and once again Psalm 3 (à 6); the composer revised them for their publication in Books IV and I respectively. The corrections made to Psalm 3 mainly concern the musical prosody. Those of Psalm 10, on the other hand, seem to be the result of purely musical considerations. Example 17 shows two corresponding fragments from the 1597 and 1604 versions of Psalm 10.

The mention of prosody leads us to the relationships between words and music. The Genevan tunes, derived from unknown sources and

Ex. 17

(a) Psalm 10 (1597)

(b) Psalm 10 (1604)

serving polystanzaic psalm translations, could not do justice to the
poetic rhythm. If they are sung monophonically, that is, free from fixed
musical metre, this deficiency need not be disturbing. The French
word-accent, being less emphatic than that of Germanic languages,
tolerates to a certain extent the shift to an unstressed position of a
normally stressed syllable; in music this is paralleled by the use of long
and short notes, length being associated (but not inevitably) with stress.

However, in a polyphonic texture with its relatively fixed musical metre, this licence becomes less acceptable. In the 'strict' cantus firmus psalms, Sweelinck could remedy the defective prosody of the prescribed melody only through a correct treatment of the poetic lines in the other parts. The 'free' cantus firmus, on the other hand, was rhythmically malleable and could be adapted to the text of each verse. Ex. 18 shows how the composer proceeded in the seven stanzas of Psalm 61 (II). The different versions include slight deviations from the given melody in verses 5 and 7 as well as an embellishment in verse 3.

Other inconveniences encountered in the psalm tunes relate to pitch. The replacement of high notes set to unstressed syllables would affect the identity of the melody. Only the frequent textual repetitions offer the possibility of melodic corrections; Sweelinck accordingly avails himself of this means on many occasions. He applies the same procedure to cantus firmus phrases whose melodic direction contradicts the sense of the words, as in Psalm 105 (Book I), line 2 (Ex. 19).

Ex. 18

Ex. 19

Elsewhere, an emphatic motif draws the attention to specific words unstressed in the neutral Genevan tune. In Psalm 88 (IV) the descending cantus firmus, set to the line 'Iour et nuict devant toy je crie', appears twice in the treble. Between this phrase and its repetition, Sweelinck inserted a motif of his own: an ascending leap of a fifth, reaching the highest note of the treble's compass, underlines the words 'je crie'. In this way the composer considerably enhanced the emotional force of the textual message. Interpolations of this kind even occur within a phrase of the pre-existent melody. In the third line of Psalm 37 (III), (Ex. 20), Sweelinck adds to the notes of the cantus firmus (marked here with crosses), a descending scale of a ninth which is subsequently imitated by the other voices. By doing so he supplies the musical image of the word 'ruine', which was lacking in the original melody.

Since the floridly metaphorical language of the psalms is re-flected in Marot's and de Bèze's poetic translations, the texts offer ample scope for musical word-painting. Melismas set to words like 'chanter', 'rire', 's'enfuir', 'chasser', 'course', 'plusieurs', 'grand nombre', 'fleuves', 'train', 'ruisseau', and 'voler' belong to the conventional devices of Sweelinck's time. The same is true of words which, though not really depicted, are nevertheless traditionally rendered by melismatic passages: 'gloire', 'regne', 'menteuses', etc. The circle or spiral is translated by its sonorous equivalent, a melisma returning to the initial note. Examples include 'autour', 'environnement', and 'vignes'. Other figures exploit musical pitch; they relate to 'hauteur', 'profondeur', 'terre et ciel' (octave leap), 'chemin' (a scale), and similar concepts. All these examples relieve the abstract character of the pre-existent melodies and contribute to the variety within the settings. Moreover, they occasionally lead to interesting contrapuntal textures as, for instance, in Psalm 93, verse 1 (IV), at the depiction of 'fleuves impetueux' and 'le son des flots tempestueux', or in Psalm 83 (IV) on 'furie grande'.

While it is true that Sweelinck's word-painting is based on convention, his personal application of the devices shows considerable ingenuity. The melismas set to 'confusion' in Psalm 53, verse 5 (IV), scatter the lines to the four winds; 'tremblez' in Psalm 4, verse 2 (III),

is depicted by trills consisting not only of seconds but even thirds and fourths. Chromaticism as a means of word-painting is very rarely employed. A touching example occurs in the double-choir Psalm 113, verse 4 (III); here, three parts imitate each other with descending semitones set to 'les povres sur terre'. On the other hand, there are several instances of words interpreted as musical concepts and rendered as such. In Psalm III, verse 4 (IV), 'accord' is set as a triad on D; in Psalm 12, verse 1 (II), 'diminués' appears as a melisma with quavers and semiquavers in the treble; and in the 'Oraison dominicale'

(III), the phrase 'Advienne tost to sainct regne parfaict' ends on a *clausula perfecta*. Musical text interpretation may even go so far as to present biblical exegesis. Psalm 19, verse 1 (III) speaks of God's works:

> Les cieux en chacun lieu
> La puissance de Dieu
> Racomptent aux humains:
> Ce grand entour espars
> Publie en toutes parts
> L'ouvrage de ses mains.

Here the word 'ouvrage' is set as a long melismatic canon between the second treble and the tenor. In this way the composer expresses the fundamental Calvinist idea that man should try to reflect, however imperfectly, the work of God. The procedure may also relate to the widespread conception of human music mirroring the harmony of the universe.

Particularly attractive are Sweelinck's musical translations of contrasting textual images. Examples include Psalm 148, verse 3 (III): '. . . au profond de voz creux' (low pitch and slow rhythm in a setting for four voices) is followed by 'Feux gresle' (lively and melismatic, high pitch); and *note bianche* set to 'neiges et glaces froides' are contrasted with *note nere* ('vents de tempestes forts'). Similarly, in the fourth verse of the same psalm, 'Bestes sur la terre rempantes' (low pitch, long note values) is answered by the three upper voices singing 'Bestes parmi le ciel volantes' (short note values and, of course, a melisma set to the last word).

In Latin psalms, the setting of the word 'laudate' as a descending arpeggiated triad was a topos applied by many composers of the time, including Monteverdi. Curiously enough, this formula occurs in one of the Genevan tunes ('Louez-le', Psalm 134). Perhaps Loys Bourgeois intentionally composed or adapted the melody in this way. Although in Sweelinck's setting (III), the free voices do not adopt the figure, in the first version of the same psalm (I) the composer does indeed use the topos abundantly in all the voices, the short note values being effectively contrasted with the breves in the bass part (Ex. 21).

As is well known, the text of Palm 150 (III) offers particularly rich musical imagery, mentioning, in addition to singing, no fewer than eight instruments. Sweelinck did not miss the opportunity to display his mastery of word-painting; to render instrumental sounds with human voices was a real challenge. For this purpose he went so far as to truncate several words. 'Harpe', stripped of its mute syllable and

62

frequently repeated, gives the impression of a plucked instrument. 'Tabour', likewise repeated, loses its first syllable, with the result that the verbal sound becomes suggestively dull ('ta-bou, bou, bour'); the effect is reinforced by a low homorhythmic setting on a single harmony. 'Phifres' are effectively depicted by melismatic passages in the two trebles, and 'orgues' through a contrapuntal device (inverted and non-inverted imitations). The trumpet being absent, the 'hautbois' appropriates its triadic motifs, and, not surprisingly, the 'musette' sounds above a pedal point. Finally, a melismatic setting of 'bourdon' (tenors and basses) suggests a low-pitched, unspecified instrument. No wonder that this piece is the most frequently performed among Sweelinck's psalms.

Sweelinck's Psalter leaves the listener, the performer, and not least the analyst, in continual astonishment. The more its display of mastery is evidenced by examples of kaleidoscope variety, the more one becomes aware of the difficulty of capturing the greatness of this work and expressing it in words. Let us therefore move on to a few questions relating to the social conditions of the time. Who sang these psalms? Where we they performed? Why did Sweelinck, a Dutch composer in a

Dutch city, prefer the French texts to one of the existing translations into his own language?

The currently favoured answer to the last question is that the composer associated with a social class which used to speak and write French on many occasions, if only to distinguish itself from the lower strata. French was considered a cultural language, Dutch merely a means of communication.

Although this explanation contains some truth, it is weakened by the fact that three Dutch Psalters had been published between 1556 and 1568. These settings, though less elaborate than those of Sweelinck, were certainly not exclusively written for the lower classes. Further, the foundation of the Republic, a few decades later, called for the use of a language common to all social strata and mirroring the new nation's identity. This was strongly felt by the intelligentsia, including the poets. Therefore it is hard to maintain that, in Sweelinck's time, Dutch was considered merely a linguistic vehicle for everyday's communication, whereas more elevated thoughts had to be expressed in French, Italian, or Latin.

Another more convincing explanation of Sweelinck's preference for a French text may be advanced. Let us assume for a moment that originally the composer considered setting a Dutch Psalter, based on the officially accepted melodies. If so, what choice did he have? Actually there was no real choice, the only current translation which fitted the tunes being that of Dathenus. Other Dutch Psalters, such as the one by Marnix van St Aldegonde, were unsuitable, because they do not observe the syllabic structure of Marot's and de Bèze's texts, inherent in the melodies. Therefore Dathenus's version was the only remaining possibility. Although prescribed by the National Synod and accepted by the population, this Psalter was strongly criticized among poets and intellectuals because of its artificial idiom and clumsy poetic expression. We need not wonder that Sweelinck rejected it. Let us not forget that he was an educated man—first schooled by the learned Buyck and afterwards probably self-taught—and that his literary taste, as shown by his secular vocal works, was highly developed. We can easily imagine that the idea of setting Dathenus's verses would not have appealed to him, nor would it have pleased his Amsterdam friends. Thus the original French Psalter was the logical choice.

The answer to the second question, that of the identity of the performers, seems obvious. Sweelinck dedicated Book II to eight 'philomuses en la tres renommee ville d'Amstelredam', who used to join their voices 'pour . . . imiter l'harmonie des esprits qui sont consommés en tres parfaict accord'. Whether or not these persons were members of the Collegium musicum, it was for Amsterdam amateur musicians that the composer wrote his Psalter. One problem, however, remains to be solved. Who sang the treble? Sigtenhorst Meyer categorically stated that the cantus and high quintus parts were performed exclusively by boys.[6] In my opinion this is very much open to question. Unlike the former Catholic churches and monasteries, the Calvinist churches did not offer any opportunity for musical education. Only in primary schools were boys and girls taught monophonic psalm singing; this hardly sufficed for the performance of Sweelinck's difficult treble parts. Therefore, rather than boys, it must have been adult females who took part in the performance of the psalms. There is ample evidence for this supposition. Women are almost always included in the groups of music-making people depicted in numerous paintings of the time. Moreover, the position of the female in liberal Dutch society allowed much more activity in social and cultural life than elsewhere. Nor were there any religious obstacles. When Calvin counselled the practice of private devotions, including psalm singing, he certainly did not want to exclude women from this *excercice spirituelle*.

As for the place of performance, I agree with Sigtenhorst Meyer that, apart from home, this must have been the church.[7] In particular, the many-voiced psalms lend themselves very well for performance in a capacious building. Besides, Sweelinck's own church offered the opportunity of using the small choir organ for the purpose of practising these difficult works. Evidence for extra-liturgical psalm singing in the Dutch churches is provided by the publication of Goudimel's homophonic psalter with Dathenus's texts underlaid; it appeared in Leyden (1620). According to the printer's foreword, this edition was strongly recommended by Sweelinck. More explicit is a passage in a letter from the French minister in The Hague, Olivier de Raffélis, addressed to Constantijn Huygens and dated 29 September 1641: 'Last Thursday Mr. Milleville tried [the newly built organ in the Kloosterkerk] for the first time in our presence, that is, ten or twelve people, and we joined our voices to the instrument, which sounded well.' Finally, it should be observed that outside the Netherlands, extra-liturgical psalm singing in Calvinist churches was far from uncommon. This is attested to by the practice of the citizens of Zuoz (Engadine), who used to sing Sweelinck's psalms in their local church until about 1840 (see p. 12).

So we may assume that the works of the Amsterdam psalmist were practised and performed in the Oude Kerk. If the performances (almost certainly by solo voices) may not have attained the perfection of those offered by today's professional ensembles, one nevertheless marvels at the vocal capacities and skill of the amateurs who sang these elaborate compositions. In our own time, such a high level of attainment by dilettanti would be unthinkable. Those who believe firmly in historical progress will have to admit that in this case their doctrine has gone into reverse.

The Latin Motets

The circumstances under which the *Cantiones sacrae* appeared in Antwerp (1619) are not entirely clear. It has been suggested that the book was printed without the composer's knowledge. Another hardly less audacious suggestion is that a few years before his death Sweelinck openly or secretly returned to the Catholic faith. Both hypotheses are very unlikely. In the course of his life the Amsterdam master had become acquainted with the musical liturgies of three different Christian churches—the Roman Catholic, the Calvinist, and the Lutheran—all of which are reflected in his work.[8] Since there is not the slightest indication that he was ever involved or even interested in controversial matters of religious orthodoxy, his adherence to the Dutch Reformed Church should be viewed in the light of the social conditions of the time; being the consequence of his official position, it certainly did not exclude sympathy for other confessions. That the dedication of the *Cantiones sacrae* to Cornelis Plemp was signed by Pierre Phalèse can be explained as a prudent move. Sweelinck, who had contributed so much to the fame of Amsterdam, had nothing to fear from the city's magistracy, but by retreating behind his publisher he may have tried to avoid irritating the more uncompromising clergymen. Yet with a single exception—the Marian antiphon 'Regina coeli'—none of the chosen texts could have offended orthodox Calvinists. Twenty-seven of the texts, including nine psalms, are taken from the Scriptures, and the remaining nine, though appearing in Roman liturgical books, are in conformity with Protestant belief. Only insiders would have known that Sweelinck made his choice of scriptural verses from the Breviary rather than the Vulgate: this is apparent from the fragments of chant melodies hidden in various motets. Finally, there is the question of whether Plemp or Phalèse himself paid for the publication of the work. The dedicatee, a man of ample means, could easily have done so, but at least one indisputable fact speaks against this assumption: by 1619 Sweelinck was an internationally renowned musician, whose works could be printed by any publisher without great financial risk. A passage in the dedication, for that matter, implicitly refers to this: '. . . velut uno Cadmeio iacto semine, copiosam aciem Exemplarium in lucem produxi'. As the Cadmean seed was in fact the teeth of the slain dragon, giving birth to an army bound for self-destruction, the simile seems rather far-fetched if not indelicate. However, the main point, that a large number of copies were printed, is clear beyond doubt.

The *Cantiones sacrae* are written for five parts, the quintus being variously a second treble and a second tenor. A novelty in Sweelinck's vocal music was the addition of a basso continuo, which actually is a *basso seguente*. The omission of this part by Seiffert in the sixth volume of the first complete edition was based on a misconception. The editor, believing firmly in the purely vocal performance of sixteenth-century sacred music, considered the chordal instrument absolutely alien to the style (*direkt stilwidrig*). However, when he came to compare Sweelinck's motets with those of Palestrina and Lassus, he overlooked the modern features, especially the 'harmonic' polyphony, which will be discussed below. Further, the instrumental bass is not always strictly identical with the lowest vocal part. Slight deviations and additions occur rather frequently: take, for example, the avoidance of parallel fifths between the *fondamento* and the treble in no. 13, 'Hodie Christus natus est' (Ex. 22).

In one instance, the continuo contains a complete untexted transcription of the vocal parts, notated on separate staves. This occurs in the *tertia pars* of no. 33, 'Regina coeli', which is the only section in the whole volume set for three parts throughout (cantus, altus, tenor). In his edition of the motets (*Opera omnia*, vi), Alfons Annegarn argued plausibly that this scoring does not constitute a realization of the thorough bass, but is intended, rather, as a point of reference for the

Ex. 22

organist, whose instrument is to remain silent during the performance of this verse. Another explanation could be that the transcription of the vocal parts was made for the purpose of practice.

The amazing compositional virtuosity displayed in Book III of the Psalms permitted no further development. This must have been the reason why, in the Latin motets, Sweelinck returned to his favourite five-part scoring. Characteristic of this *opus ultimum* is the liberty the composer allowed himself. Neither specific texts nor pre-existent melodies restrict his freedom of expression. Ingenious contrapuntal devices, though employed occasionally, are no longer to the fore. Obviously, Sweelinck no longer felt the need to display his skill in this field; instead, he concentrated on other aspects, in particular a subtle and penetrating rendering of the verbal message. The few borrowings of pre-existent melodic material are handled freely. Only one piece, 'Regina coeli', is heavily dependent on the chant melody, but even here we find slight deviations as well as melismatic elaborations (Ex. 23). While the mode in this motet, the sixth, is the same as that of the antiphon, the 'Te Deum' (no. 37), being written in the first mode transposed, differs from the chant, which is in the third mode. The melody of verse 20 appears in the treble of Sweelinck's *quarta pars* (Ex. 24).

Other rather arbitrary borrowings are little more than allusions, occurring in the opening bars or in the middle of the pieces. Examples include the settings of the Beatitudes (no. 6); the Magnificat antiphons 'Petite et accipietis' and 'Gaude et laetare' (no. 15 and 18, the latter borrowing fragments of the melody contained in the 1561 Amsterdam *Cantuale*); and finally Simeon's words 'Nunc dimittis servum tuum' in no. 30 ('Hodie beata virgo Maria'; melody in the tenor).

The relative modernity of texture in this late collection is apparent from the frequent homophony. Far from being chordal middle voices, the inner parts of these fragments, which often cross, have a strong melodic profile. Nevertheless, Sweelinck's homophony seems more harmonically inspired in these motets than in the psalms (with the exception of the many-voiced pieces from Books III and IV). The homophonic passages sometimes serve to express doctrinal statements, for example, 'Spiritus sanctus . . . vos docebit omnia' in no. 23 ('Paracletus autem'), and '. . . sanctum quoque paracletum spiritum' (no. 37, 'Te Deum laudamus', *secunda pars*). The last-named motet, which concludes the volume, is full of impressive homophonic fragments, for instance its final psalm quotation, 'In te Domine speravi' (the same text, Psalm 30, is set as no. 4; there extended to

Ex. 23

(e)

Al – le – lu – – – – – ia:

(Altus)

Al – le – – – – – – – lu – ia.

(f)

O – ra pro no – bis De – um,

(Cantus)

O – ra pro_____ no – bis De – um,

(g)

Al – – – – – – – – le – lu – ia.

(Quintus)

Al – le – – – – – – – – – lu – ia.

Ex. 24

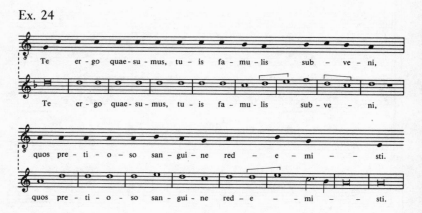

Te er – go quae-su – mus, tu – is fa – mu – lis sub – ve – ni,

Te er – go quae-su – mus, tu – is fa – mu – lis sub – ve – ni,

quos pre – ti – o – so san – gui – ne red – e – mi – – sti.

quos pre – ti – o – so san – gui – ne red – e – mi – – sti.

70

verse 6). Many homophonic passages also occur in the setting of Psalm 129, 'De profundis clamavi' (no. 29). The extremely low-pitched opening (*a* in the treble and *D* in the bass) treats the text imitatively, but there then follows a high homorhythmic setting of 'Domine, exaudi vocem meam'. The second verse ends by descending from the highest note *f"* to *a* below middle C. In the course of the piece short homophonic and polyphonic sections alternate continuously.

Another modern trait is the 'harmonic' polyphony, which often results from paired voices imitating each other. A characteristic example is the opening of no. 32, 'Gaudete omnes', which is set to a free text (Ex. 25). Similar examples are found in no. 3 ('Ab oriente'), bars 68 ff.; no. 12 ('Iusti autem'), bars 10 ff.; and in several concluding Alleluyas which, curiously enough, nearly always receive a syllabic setting.

In his otherwise perceptive description of the *Cantiones sacrae*, Sigtenhorst Meyer mentioned the almost complete absence of madrigalisms, which 'would not suit sacred songs of this quality'.[9] Both the statement and the argument are wrong. Madrigalisms occur as abundantly in the motets as in the previous works; the composer hardly misses an opportunity to apply this device. As regards the argument, in Sweelinck's time, word-painting had no strict secular

Ex. 25

connotation. On the contrary, it was generally considered to reinforce the devotional expression of sacred texts. There is, in the composer's motets, a tendency towards a more subtle illustration of the words than in the secular compositions. Apart from the conventional application of madrigalisms (a high note on 'caelum', an octave leap on 'clamavi', a melisma on 'cantate', black notation on 'noctem' etc.), we find particularly ingenious and elaborate examples of more subtle word-painting. In the setting of Psalm 127 (no. 28, 'Beati omnes'), Sweelinck renders the words 'qui ambulant in viis eius' by the image of people walking in various directions. 'Labores' are depicted by melismas, while 'vitis' (vine) and 'in circuitu' are rendered by the musical equivalent of a circle. The word 'pacem' checks the preceding flow of minims and semiminims; its two syllables are homorhythmically set on a breve and a semibreve, introducing a moment of quietness. Examples in other motets include the setting of 'intrabit in regnum coelorum' (no. 1, 'Non omnis'). The ascending scale of semibreves in the bass, though effective, is rather conventional, but the other voices convey the original image of people climbing a ladder (Ex. 26).

'Ubi duo vel tres' (no. 27) opens with the cantus and altus only, the second imitating the first by inversion; in bar 3, however, they are joined by the quintus, and all three voices homorhythmically sing 'vel tres'. Descending and ascending melodies set to the seventh verse of the Magnificat (no. 34) seem almost clichéd; but in this instance, the

Ex. 26

words 'Deposuit potentes de sede' and 'et exaltavit humiles' are sung
simultaneously until the 'humiles', leaving the 'potentes' silent, reach
their highest note (a''). A more exceptional case is the sudden slowing
down of the rhythm at the words 'expectatio nostra' (no. 32, 'Gaudete
omnes'). The same device is applied to 'quia' in no. 16 ('Euge serve
bone').

73

As in the psalms, chromaticism is used only sparingly, but a few examples achieve a meaningful illustration of the words in question. In no. 20 ('De profundis'), a chromatic half-scale is set to 'ex omnibus iniquitates eius'. This ascending melody, denoting anxiety, spans the fifth C–G but lacks the semitones between C and D as well as between E and F sharp. However, a fully chromatic fourth is encountered in the *quinta pars* of the 'Te Deum' (no. 37). It appears, imitated by several other parts, both in an ascending and descending form, thus expressing fear as well as sorrow (Ex. 27). The former connotation should be seen in the light of the preceding verse: 'Dignare, Domine, die isto sine peccato nos custodire'; here the word 'peccato' is also illustrated through chromaticism. The chordal juxtapositions in Ex.27 are striking, but should not be taken as a harmonically daring procedure. They result from the melodic chromaticism. On the other hand, the double suspensions occurring in no. 19 ('Qui vult venire post me') provoke sharp dissonances which are undoubtedly intended as such; the text 'et tollat crucem suam' speaks for itself (Ex. 28).[10]

A consideration of the *Cantiones sacrae* reveals a prevalence of joyful and jubilant motets. Even emotionally neutral texts are enlivened by concluding Alleluya sections. Alleluyas also occur in the middle of two pieces: 'Regina coeli' (no. 33) and 'Hodie Christus natus est' (no. 13). While in the Marian antiphon these interruptions, contained in the liturgical text, are obligatory, in the Magnificat antiphon for the

Ex. 27

75

Ex. 28

Nativity they were not only added specially by the composer but were also complemented by a repeated call: 'Noe, Noe'. The latter motet is particularly interesting because of its formal qualities. Sweelinck makes use of the threefold occurrence of the word 'hodie' to create a rondo-like form. As the opening motif is first sung by the tenor solo and then homorhythmically taken over by the four other parts, this refrain is set as a miniature responsory. Its dance-like rhythm effectively contrasts with that of the intermediate sections (Ex. 29).

Despite their jubilant tone, Sweelinck's motets are relatively intimate works, lacking any trace of the magnificence and splendour displayed in several psalms of the 1614 volume. This is even true of the concluding 'Te Deum laudamus' which, though impressive, touches us as much by the delicate treatment of several textual details as by the homophonic expression of faith. In this respect, a comparison of two different settings of another text, sharing a common opening motif, is very instructive. I am referring to a passage from Psalm 17 ('Diligam te'). The first setting (*a*) occurs in the *Cantiones sacrae* (no. 6), the second (*b*) in the spectacular eight-part *Canticum in honorem nuptiarum Johannis Stoboei* (1617), already mentioned in the previous chapter (Ex. 30).

In Sweelinck's motets we find practically all the compositional procedures employed during his lifetime, fused with modern traits. It is the work of a man possessing a sovereign command of his craft which enables him to arrive at a synthesis of different stylistic elements

Ex. 29

78

Ex. 30

(a)

80

developed during the era of the high Renaissance. An observation by Gustave Reese, which is often quoted, may suitably conclude this chapter: 'With Sweelinck the great production of the Netherlands in the field of vocal polyphony comes to an end. It does not wane ignominiously, however, but closes in a brilliant and noble sunset.'[11]

IV
INSTRUMENTAL MUSIC

Sweelinck's Instruments

The large organ in the Oude Kerk was built by Henrick Niehoff (with the occasional assistance of his brother Herman) and Hans van Coelen (Cologne). The work began in 1539 and was finished in 1542. Since an extensive article by Cornelis Edskes about the instrument and its small companion (the choir organ, also built by Niehoff, with Jasper Janszoon) is included in Curtis's book, only a few data need to be mentioned here.[1] Both the large and the small organ were rebuilt as soon as 1567–8 by Pieter Janszoon de Swart of Utrecht. The specification of the choir organ as it was in Sweelinck's lifetime includes the following divisions: the *Principael* (Great) with nine, the *Borstwerck* with three, and the *Pedael* with one stop. As for the large organ, its *Positijf achter den rug* (*Rückpostiv*) had ten, its *Principael* four, its '*Boven int werck*' (*Oberwerk*) nine, and its *Pedael* two stops. The latter instrument with a keyboard for each division was famous not only in the Dutch Republic but also in Germany and the Southern Netherlands. In the surviving contract of the 1682 reconstruction it is called 'one of the best in Christendom'.

The compass of the keyboards, especially that of the *Principael*, is a matter of controversy. While experts agree that a'' was the highest note, the lowest was, according to Vente and Klotz, F'.[2] Edskes, on the other hand, believes that the compass extended downwards only to F. The basis for assuming the presence of the particularly low note is a passage in the 1539 contract which speaks of a range of 'up to four octaves'; this, however, could mean merely that it would exceed three octaves. A still stronger argument against the F' is that the 1682 contract stipulated an extension in both directions; that is, from a'' to c''' and from 'F nederwaerts tot C'. If we read for F and C the symbols F' and C' respectively, this would have produced a total range of five octaves, which seems most unlikely. Yet Edskes's argument also contains a weak point; his restricted compass precludes the performance of several low notes present in Sweelinck's works. His suggestion that the pieces in question were probably intended for harpsichord performance is anything but convincing, as they include chorale settings and echo fantasias which do not fit plucked keyboard instruments. So the matter remains unsettled.

The harpsichord of Sweelinck's time was a single-manual instrument with one eight-foot and one four-foot stop (or, less frequently built, two eight-foot stops). Its compass was about four octaves (*C–c'''* or *C–a''*). Virginals were built mainly in two types differentiated by tone colour. The more popular was the one with the keyboard on the right, the *muselaer*. The other type, with the keyboard on the left, was called the spinet (the polygonal Italian *spinetta* was hardly known in the Northern Netherlands). Sweelinck was certainly familiar with the double virginal, the so-called 'mother and child', which combined a normal with a superposable octave instrument; these were produced as early as 1580 by Flemish builders including Hans Ruckers.

During Sweelinck's lifetime the standard six-course lute became extended with a seventh pair of strings. This is shown by the additional line in the tablatures of the Thysius Manuscript (*c.*1590–*c.*1625). Moreover, the bass strings are mentioned in one of the most famous Dutch songbooks, the *Neder-landtsche Gedenckclanck* by Adrianus Valerius (Haarlem, 1626). This chronicle of the insurrection against the King of Spain includes a large number of patriotic songs—among them the one which has become the Dutch national anthem—together with their intabulations for lute and cittern. In view of the low notes that appear in his lute pieces, Sweelinck very probably played an instrument with seven or more courses.

Stylistic Characteristics and Historical Background

The style of Sweelinck's keyboard works is marked mainly by two different techniques: contrapuntal elaboration of thematic material and the use of idiomatic figuration. As with other composers of early instrumental music, the counterpoint is rooted in sixteenth-century vocal genres, notably the Netherlands motet. The devices found in Sweelinck's own vocal works (free imitation, strict imitation, imitation by inversion, augmentation, diminution, the combination of theme and countersubjects written in invertible counterpoint, etc.) likewise appear in his instrumental music. The absence of restricting factors, such as the text and the range of the human voice, may account for the extension of melodic liberty as well as the more frequently occurring sequential passages. Nevertheless, the contrapuntal procedures employed in the Psalter and those applied to the keyboard works are essentially the same.

Unlike counterpoint, Sweelinck's figurational technique is of purely instrumental origin and its provenance is less easy to determine. True, the composer's debt to the English school of virginalists (and organists) is beyond doubt, but let us not forget that the English technique itself owed much to Italian and Spanish music of the mid-sixteenth century. Nor can the possibility be entirely excluded that influences from the last two countries acted directly on the Netherlands. Curtis has shown that several items from the only Dutch keyboard source prior to Sweelinck, the so-called Susanne van Soldt Manuscript, contain specific Italian features, whereas English elements are almost completely absent.[3] As for Spain, we know that Antonio de Cabezón visited the Low Countries twice (between 1548 and 1551 as well as between 1554 and 1556). Admittedly, this does not amount to much, but it is clear that the question of the provenance of Sweelinck's idiomatic keyboard style cannot be answered unequivocally. The same is true of another question: who influenced whom? Since almost all the surviving works appear to date from the last two decades of the composer's life, it has tacitly been assumed that similar pieces written before his fortieth year were of inferior quality. However, it is very unlikely that as early as 1593 Peter Philips would have called the Amsterdam master 'an excellent man of his faculties' solely on the grounds of his brilliant playing. On the other hand, Sigtenhorst Meyer went too far when he emphasized Sweelinck's impact on his English contemporaries, playing down to a certain extent their influence on him.[4] Obviously, the biographer's underlying thought was that a composer's eminence is measured by his originality and that influences received by him detract from his greatness. A more modern view of history shows, rather, that the opposite is true. Generally speaking, the genius is not a pioneer, nor is the pioneer a genius. While the contributions to the development of Western music made by the Caccinis, Stamitzes, and Saties are truly invaluable, the greatest figures have always been those who fully realized the possibilities contained in their forerunners' innovations. Sweelinck is no exception to this rule. He could hardly have become the founder of the German school of organists, had he not subjected the stylistic elements available in his time to a strict reorganization.

It is this reorganization which struck and even shocked early researchers, whose conceptions were still informed by Romantic aesthetics. Both André Pirro and Charles van den Borren saw in

Sweelinck first of all a great musical architect, a cerebral constructor. While the latter deplored the composer's alleged lack of spontaneity and sensibility, calling him 'un génie hautain et professoral', the former thought that the fantasias would interest the mathematician rather than the true music lover.[5] Post-war studies tended to take the opposite standpoint. Willi Apel, as well as Robert Tusler, considered Sweelinck to be a master of detail, his overall form showing whimsicality and lack of coherence.[7] Neither the one nor the other view do justice to Sweelinck's compositional technique. All the elements he borrowed from his predecessors or contemporaries were made subservient to his desire for a solid structure, including the 'whimsical' figuration which often contains hidden motifs derived from the thematic material. The composer's variation technique, undoubtedly influenced by that of the English keyboard masters, was likewise reorganized, with a special concern for continuity. Moreover, Sweelinck's instrumental music shows a particularly ingenious handling of time factors. After a discussion of the five different genres (fantasias, echo fantasies, toccatas, variation cycles on sacred tunes, settings and variations on secular tunes) and a brief note on the lute pieces, we will return to Sweelinck's treatment of time factors, which reveals the inner structure of the works more clearly than traditional analysis.

The Fantasias

The classification of early keyboard genres by music historians past and present has the advantage of clarity, but its chosen nomenclature does not conform to the loose sixteenth-century practice. A polythematic imitative composition is generally called a 'ricercar', while the name 'fantasia' is reserved for monothematic pieces of the same kind. However, these two terms were originally less generic than is assumed nowadays. Rather, their respective use seems to have been more or less dependent on geographic location. In Italy the term 'fantasia' was much less current than 'ricercar', whereas the opposite was true of Spain and the northern countries. The matter is further complicated by the occurrence of the terms 'capriccio' and 'canzona' (the second in so far as it is not based on a pre-existing chanson). The only thing we can be sure of is that all the keyboard compositions provided with one of these names are among the ancestors of the fugue.

However, the distinction between monothematic and polythematic pieces is historically important, since it was Sweelinck's achievement to arrive at a synthesis of the two subgenres. Among the earliest polythematic, motet-like ricercars are those by Girolamo Cavazzoni (1543); the first monothematic piece is found in Jacob Buus's *Recercari . . . da cantare et sonare d'organo et altri stromenti* (1547). Composers from the second half of the century cultivated these two types alongside each other. Since almost all their preserved works were published posthumously, it is far from easy to establish the chronology of newly invented devices. Yet Andrea Gabrieli may be considered Sweelinck's immediate forerunner, since he seems to have been the first to add a countersubject to the principal ricercar theme, developing it to a certain extent, for instance by inversion. The Amsterdam composer may have known Gabrieli's organ works through the lost original editions, published between 1560 and 1575, or their reprints (1593, 1595, and 1596). Sweelinck could also have been familiar with the posthumous publications of Annibale Padovano, Claudio Merulo, and Sperindio Bertoldo, all of whom worked as organists in the Veneto. On the other hand, his acquaintance with the ricercars of the Neapolitan composers Rocco Rodio and Antonio Valenta seems less likely. As for the English contemporaries, he certainly knew the fantasias of Peter Philips and John Bull, and perhaps also those of William Byrd. The formal organization of these works has little affinity with that of Sweelinck's pieces, however. Only the figurational technique shows some relationship.

Sweelinck's fantasias are built on a single theme which nearly always remains unchanged throughout the piece, except for proportional treatment and occasional inversion. Out of eleven authentic works, eight show the following characteristics. Various countersubjects are set against the theme, their number ranging from three to twelve. In addition, the theme is presented together with extensive figurational passages which may conceal motifs from previously exposed melodic material. The overall form is in three large sections, the proportional lengths of which correspond more or less to the ratio 2:1:1. Exceptions include the bipartite L5[7] (the Hexachord Fantasia) whose proportions are 3:2, and L3 (the Fitzwilliam Fantasia), which has three sections of equal length. It should be observed that the prevailing tripartite form is revealed by analysis rather than performance. Unlike the nineteenth-century sonata form with its caesuras separating exposition, development, and recapitulation, the outlines of the sections contained in Sweelinck's fantasias are obscured by overlapping melodic material, interrupted cadences, or other devices *d'inganno*, which strongly enhance the overall continuity. An abstract description of the fantasia's formal disposition can be given, however:

Section I. Imitative exposition of the theme (T) combined with a countersubject (CS. 1) during the second entry and possibly another one (CS. 2) during the third entry. Theme and countersubjects are written in invertible counterpoint. In a second fugal exposition, the theme is combined with a new countersubject, and so on. One of the expositions presents the theme in stretto.

Section II. The theme is exposed in twofold augmentation and set against a new countersubject, a figurational melody, or both. This may be followed by a similar procedure applied to the theme in fourfold augmentation. Between the expositions there is at least one episode in which a new countersubject is treated in stretto before being joined to the theme.

Section III. The theme now appears in twofold diminution, either in a 'fugal' exposition or in stretto. The elaboration of the theme in halved note values is followed by its fourfold, and possibly even its eightfold diminution. In the last case the theme merges rhythmically with the figuration prevailing in the concluding section, which in this way assumes the character of a toccata. No new countersubjects are added to the theme, but towards the end it may reappear in its original form. The piece ends on a plagal cadence with brilliant scales of semiquavers or demisemiquavers.

Although each of the eight fantasias in question (L1–8) possesses its own characteristics, the above scheme is largely applicable to the analysis of all of them. A typical example of Sweelinck's handling of the theme and the countersubjects during the first exposition in Section I can be seen in a fragment from L1, the Chromatic Fantasia (Ex. 31).

Theoretically the three elements (T., CS. 1, and CS. 2) can be combined in six different ways. The composer uses five of these; from bottom to top: T.–CS. 2–CS. 1 (occurring three times, T. starting on *d*, *a*, and *e*); T.–CS. 1–CS. 2 (once, T. on *a*); CS. 1–T.–CS. 2 (twice, T. on *a* and *d'*); CS. 1–CS. 2–T. (once, T. on *e''*); and CS. 2–CS. 1–T.

Ex. 31

87

(once, T. on *a'*). As Sigtenhorst Meyer has shown, the sixth combination (CS. 2–T.–CS. 1), producing unresolved 6/4 chords, is impossible in practice.

In the Chromatic Fantasia (197 bars), the principal theme (a descending scale of five semitones covering a fourth and preceded by a canzona-like, dactylic presentation of its initial note) occurs no less than fifty times integrally and five times incompletely, that is, with one or two missing semitones. Still more amazing is the fact that among these occurrences there is not a single literal repeat. Moreover, the theme is combined with seven countersubjects, four of which are maintained for 51, 46, 22, and 25 bars respectively.

The ingenious contrapuntal elaborations in the Chromatic Fantasia, achieving a structural balance otherwise unknown in Sweelinck's time, could hardly be surpassed. Yet the work is equalled by several other compositions, including the 'Fitzwilliam' and Hexachord Fantasias (L3 and L5). The first piece is marked by the almost complete absence of countersubjects, every procedure being dependent on the theme, the longest in Sweelinck's fantasias, which consists of three phrases (Ex. 32). The opening bars also differ from those of other fantasias, the integral theme being answered both by inversion and in stretto (Ex. 33).

Ex. 32

Ex. 33

During the first section (83 bars) Sweelinck displays an almost acrobatic manipulation of the theme's three phrases, combining them in double counterpoint, both literal and inverted. The second seems to open as a simple bicinium, the augmented theme being set against a free figurational melody. However, when this is followed by a similar tricinium (bars 102 ff.), it appears that theme and figuration were written in double counterpoint; both of these not only change places but are also inverted and joined by a free middle voice. Here we have a clear instance of the figuration's integration into the structure of the piece, a compositional technique unknown to Sweelinck's contemporaries, Italian as well as English. The opening bars of both the bicinium and tricinium are given in Ex. 34 (*a*) and (*b*).

Ex. 34

The concluding section of the 'Fitzwilliam' Fantasia (bars 163 ff.) consists of two contrasting divisions. The first of these shows that the contrapuntal possibilities contained in the composite theme were far from exhausted. Instead of the expected fourfold augmentation the subject's first phase appears in the unusual proportion 3:1, against which the other voices present a stretto of the same melody in twofold diminution, first in its literal form and subsequently inverted (Ex. 35). In a second stretto (bars 184 ff.) the voices answer each other at the distance of a crochet instead of the former minim. This is followed by a third stretto based on the theme's second phrase, which is likewise presented both in its original configuration as well as inverted (bars 190 ff.). Finally, a fourth stretto treats the melody's last phrase, first virtually in the same way and then by alteration of paired voices. In the concluding division, the (bars 219–43) the reins are loosened. Against the partly abridged theme, various countervoices display attractive figurations culminating in the penultimate bar with a trill on the fifth with the semitone below. This toccata-like division opens with an upper pedal point of eight and a half tied semibreves, showing that at least in this case, performance on an organ is highly preferable to that on a harpsichord.

The fame of the Chromatic, 'Fitzwilliam', and Hexachord Fantasias—the last-named to be discussed below—seems to have detracted from interest in other works of this kind. Yet L2, L4, L6, and L7 are hardly less impressive or less ingenious with regard to thematic elaboration. Both L4 and L6 are built on themes that include non-diatonic semitones; this leads in the course of the pieces to the use of the complete chromatic fourth (descending in L4 and ascending in L6). The austere L2 is the longest of all the fantasias (317 bars). Its theme appears in twofold and fourfold augmentation as well as diminution. The presentation in breves and semibreves occurs successively in the treble (on e''), the alto (on a'), the tenor (on e'), and the bass (on a). The last entry, entailing an extremely slow harmonic rhythm, poses a problem which the composer solves by setting against the theme a number of small motifs answered in echo. Another peculiarity of this fantasia is that its subject appears in two variants, the second adopting three notes from the *dux* and seven from the *comes*. The theme of L7, too, is presented in two different versions; moreover, its rhythm changes occasionally in a way faintly reminiscent of canzonas by Trabaci and Mayone (Ex. 36).

Ex. 36

91

Apart from the theme's multiform occurrence, L7 is written entirely in the manner of the first six works. Its unusual title (*Ricercare*) may be explained by the fact that the manuscripts surviving in Turin and Padua were copied by South German scribes. L8 is not only the most simple of Sweelinck's fantasias but also the shortest (128 bars). Its theme, a diatonically descending scale covering a fifth and preceded by a canzona-like dactyl, is presented on the notes D, F, G, A, and C. Only during the last 25 bars does this melody appear in proportional forms, the usual sequence being reversed: that is, diminution preceding augmentation. As the piece is written throughout for three voices, it may well have been included in Samuel Scheidt's lost edition (1630, see p. 13).

The Hexachord Fantasia (L5) differs from the works discussed above by its opening: a countersubject precedes the theme, which does not appear until bar 6. More significant is the absence of augmented versions of the theme: hence the piece's bipartite disposition. Despite these formal divergences, the work is written in a style conforming to that of the other fantasias. Comparison with contemporary settings of the same subject shows that Sweelinck employs an entirely different technique. John Bull's three hexachord fantasias, though differing among themselves, have practically nothing in common with the composition of the Dutchman. No. 18 (in the *Musica Britannica* edition of 1960) presents the scale ut–re–mi–fa–sol–la in the ascending form, followed by the descending form twenty-three times as a *hexachordum durum* in the treble. The extremely brilliant counter-figuration marks this work a keyboard *étude*. The five-part setting, no. 19, handles the theme more freely in a particularly dense texture. The most stupendous treatment of the subject is found in no. 17. Its first presentation (ascending as well as descending on *g*) is followed by five others, each of which starts a whole tone higher than the previous one (*g–a–b–c'* sharp–*e'* flat–*f'*). Next, a similar series of six (!) entries is built on the notes *A* flat–*B* flat–*c–d–e–f* sharp. As a result the hexachord is stated on all the semitones within the octave, a feature which, in view of the restricted possibilities inherent in the temperaments used around 1600, has puzzled many a musicologist. The most plausible explanation is that the piece was composed for performance on an *arcicembalo*.[8] However this may be, Sweelinck's handling of the hexachord is almost the antithesis of Bull's. The complete theme (including both the ascending and descending scales) appears twenty-seven times, choosing for *ut* the notes F (in three octaves) or C (in two octaves) exclusively. In the course of the piece it is combined with six successive countersubjects; entries 1–5 with CS. 1; 6–7 with CS. 2; 8 with CS. 3; 9–12 (in halved note-values) with CS. 4; 13–14 (likewise diminished) with CS. 5; and 15–17 (in fourfold diminution) with CS. 6. As in the other fantasias, the last division does not introduce any new countersubjects. Instead, the theme maintaining the previous proportion is combined with figuration and treated in stretto (entries 18–20). Finally it appears in eightfold diminution, that is, in quavers (21–7). By then the original austere hexachord has been transformed into a playful motif which the composer nevertheless handles in a learned way: it is repeatedly stated in simultaneous *motu recto* and *motu contrario*. The work ends with brilliant figuration including the augmented Lydian fourth leading to the fifth in the final chord. Paradoxically, the rigorous treatment of the melodic material, characteristic of Sweelinck's procedures, results in a particularly rich content. As with the previously discussed fantasias, the technical description reveals nothing of the work's stunning beauty. One should simply listen or, still better, play.

Such are the variants occurring in the common type of Sweelinck's fantasias. The three remaining compositions are of a different order. L10, a piece in the transposed first mode of only 44 bars, is not a fantasia in the historical sense but a simple bicinium, probably written for pedagogical purposes. This little work presents a series of short two-part canons, some of which end with a regular cadence, while others are connected without any caesura. The scheme is shown in Table 1.

TABLE 1

Bars	Answer	Distance	Closing	Cadence
1 –14	lower 8th	semibreve	linked	—
14–20	upper 11th	minim	free	B flat
20– 6	lower 8th	minim	linked	—
26–34	upper 5th	minim	free	D
34– 7	lower 8th	minim	linked	—
37–44	lower 8th	crotchet	free	G

L9 and L32* show ostinato technique co-ordinated with imitative treatment of melodic elements. Both works open with a long section in which the continually repeated theme is set against a toccata-like free voice. This is followed by a setting of the ostinato melody joined with short countersubjects and embedded in various figurational passages.

Finally, a four-part texture treats the theme, literally as well as diminutively, both in stretto and in combination with new counter-subjects. The gradual increase in the number of voices determines the overall structure of these two works. Typical of Sweelinck's procedures is the handling of the ostinato principle in L9. The theme appears successively in three voices: bass, treble, and alto. Each of these presents the melody 3 × 3 times, that is, with threefold entries on D, G, and A respectively.[9] However, the imaginative interplay of theme, countersubjects, and figuration throughout the two ostinato divisions betrays nothing of this internal arithmetic organization. L32* shows more freedom in the treatment of its musical components. The theme's second half appears several times between the ostinato repetitions of the complete melody. Yet the strettos, starting already in the middle section, display considerable contrapuntal ingenuity. The theme is answered both at the distance of a breve and at that of a semibreve. During its presentation in halved note-values this device is carried even further, the respective distances being a dotted semibreve, a minim, and a crochet. The mere occurrence of this contrapuntal feat bears the infallible mark of Sweelinck; therefore, the attribution of the anonymous manuscript to him is more than plausible.

Among the instrumental works of the Amsterdam organist, the fantasias are those written on the largest scale. No previous or contemporary composer ever achieved the harmonious synthesis of unity and variety shown in these powerful creations. Moreover, Sweelinck's fantasia already contains all the elements of the baroque fugue, the development of which would be unthinkable without him.

The Echo Fantasias

Sweelinck's four authentic works employing the technique of echo are usually termed fantasia, just as they were in the seventeenth century. Nevertheless, these pieces are only loosely related to the monothematic compositions discussed in the previous section. The apparent resemblance goes no further than to the division into three main sections, the first of which is predominantly written in a polyphonic style, while the last assumes the character of a toccata. Yet the tripartite form of the echo fantasias is much more sharply delineated than that of the 'fugal' fantasias; the sections of the former end on cadences without any melodic overlap. The main difference, however, is the lack of a theme determining the overall structure. The 'abstract' disposition of the pieces may be described as follows:

Section I. Several consecutive melodies (more or less profiled) are treated imitatively or canonically in two or more voices. A free voice occasionally imitating the melody is added to this texture. Towards the end, short motifs repeated at various intervals announce the succeeding echo section.

Section II consists mainly of motifs answered by echo. The answer is either at the same pitch or at the lower octave. Change of harmony mostly occurs on the last note of the echo. The motif never spans more than one bar; its harmonization is occasionally adopted by the answer (two- or three-part echoes). Both the unison and octave echoes are to be performed with a contrasting soft tone-colour implying the use of at least two manuals. This is also true of pseudo-echoes, that is, answers occurring at other intervals, which are often found in sequential passages. An accelerated treatment of the echo may result in a stretto.

Section III is written in toccata style and includes the use of motifs repeated at the lower octave or other intervals.

The first piece, L11, largely follows this scheme. A long canon at the octave between the lowest and the upper middle voice (bars 4–20; the soprano enters only at bar 28) is followed by several others. From bar 52 onwards a number of motifs answered by pseudo-echoes, prefigure the central section of the fantasia. However, before this point is reached, there is another subsection written in canonic and free imitative style, involving the two middle voices as well as the lower-middle and the upper voice. The first section of the piece closes on a cadence at bar 79, marking a caesura. Section II opens with short motifs answered literally or at various other intervals, but the series of true echoes begins only at bar 89. These are mostly at the same pitch as their antecedents and are marked in the source (Liège, Bibliothèque de l'Université, MS 888) with red ink. Whereas in some cases the frequently occurring sequential passages affect the character of the echo, in others they leave it untouched. The difference lies in the length of the sequential chain links. If each of them spans both the motif and its softly played repeat, the latter will be a true echo. If, however, the link comprises only the antecedent, the consequent inevitably becomes a pseudo-echo, occurring at the upper or lower step of the scale. Ex. 37 shows the application of the first procedure followed by the second. Section III, which is also separated from the foregoing section by an unequivocal cadence, opens exceptionally with a short 'fugal' division, but from bar 174 until the end the writing is completely in the style of a toccata. This final division includes several echoes, both at the octave and at 'irregular' intervals.

95

Ex. 37

L12, running to 106 bars only, may have been shortened by the scribe of the sole existing manuscript (Berlin, Stadtbibliothek). If so, he preserved the overall tripartite form, which only differs from that of the preceding piece by its smooth connection of the middle echo section with the concluding toccata section. A remarkable passage occurs in bars 44–9: a motif and its echo are presented as a sequence on a chromatic bass, first ascending, then descending, and finally blossoming into a two-part canon. When, at bar 62, the echoes reappear, the usual order of pitch is reversed, the motifs occurring in the bass and the answers at the higher octave. Otherwise the piece is written, despite its restricted dimensions, in accordance with the above scheme.

L13, the longest of the four fantasias, has only octave echoes. Several of them include not only the melody but also the harmony of the foregoing motif (Ex. 38). The extended concluding section fuses toccata figuration with echo technique, which entails a particularly slow harmonic rhythm: during the last 47 bars there are only twelve chord changes. Like L11, the piece is of a high quality.

The last echo fantasia (L14) is again a short composition; in this case the restricted dimensions must be considered authentic, the work being preserved in three manuscripts. Its overall form differs from that of the other pieces by having an exceptionally long introductory section (100 bars); the ensuing echo and toccata sections run to only 21 bars each. Moreover, the cadence separating the last two is overlapped by scales. The striking acceleration of the canonic rhythm, occurring in bars 52 ff., will be discussed in the last part of this chapter.

Was Sweelinck the inventor of the echo fantasia? In the past this has

96

been tacitly assumed, but recently some doubts have arisen. L34*, a work of high quality, which formally was considered to be a composition of the Amsterdam master (mainly because of the initials J. P. appearing in one of the two sources), can no longer be attributed to him with certainty. The opening contrapuntal section is very short (only 12 bars); its theme is subsequently presented with echo, and from this point on, the alternation of loud and soft passages continues until the end. Several characteristics are quite alien to the style of the four authentic works: the length of the motifs (some of which exceed four bars), the complete absence of octave echoes, and the fact that the echo occasionally *precedes* its 'antecedent'. Leonhardt believes the piece to have been composed by a south German master; his suggestion that it is an arrangement of an instrumental double-choir work seems, however, rather far-fetched.[10]

One might wonder why the Venetian organists did not cultivate this genre. In Italian madrigals, early operas, and even sacred music, echoed phrases are often encountered; for instance, in Monteverdi's *Orfeo* and his Marian Vespers. The answer to the question is that the

Ex. 38

restricted dimensions of the Italian organs precluded the use of echo effects. It is significant that the large organ in St Mark's, though at the time considered one of the best in Italy, was only a single-manual instrument with nine stops.[11] This means that it was even smaller than the choir organ in the Amsterdam Oude Kerk!

The echo fantasia did not develop after Sweelinck's death. Neither his pupils nor any other baroque composer took an interest in it, so the genre simply vanished.

The Toccatas

It may be assumed that among Sweelinck's keyboard works quite a few were intended as studies for his pupils. A typical compositional exercise is the *Praeludium pedaliter* (L27), which shows the employment of the harmonic or contrapuntal suspension. This device is applied no less than ninety-two times within a piece running to 95 bars. While this separate item does not fit into any category, the twelve preserved toccatas belong to a distinct genre, serving technical ends of keyboard playing. The almost calculated display of virtuosic patterns, such as scales, triadic motifs, trills, and quickly repeated notes—often alternating between the right and the left hand—points to them having been written for pedagogical purposes. Indications of fingering in several manuscript sources also show the instructional character of these pieces. A few short and relatively easy toccatas were probably intended for amateurs. On the other hand, particularly elaborate works like L15–17 may have been composed for concert performance. In general, the toccatas are suited both to the organ and the harpsichord.

Although no specific model can be traced, Sweelinck must have found the ingredients of his toccatas in the works of Venetian organists of the late sixteenth century. Significantly, it was not the most outstanding among them, Claudio Merulo, who influenced the Dutchman. The sectional contrasts, brilliant passage-work, and unpredictable changes of texture in Merulo's toccatas, foreshadowing Frescobaldi, are quite alien to Sweelinck's style. On the other hand, the more rationally organized *toccate* and *intonationi* by Andrea Gabrieli offered possibilities of development. The way in which Sweelinck transformed Gabrieli's rather stale idiom is quite characteristic of his compositional technique. Instead of unimaginative mechanical scales, he employs elaborate figuration; distinct motifs emanating from preceding material are presented in sequential form, and the application of continuity devices neutralizes the mosaic-like juxtaposition of separate elements. Like his fantasias, Sweelinck's toccatas reveal their cunning inner organization only through analysis. When performed, they give the impression of spontaneity: a true *composition* is presented as if it were an extemporization.

The slow opening bars of these works have been described as being either chordal or imitative; this, however, does not take into account that in most cases the chords contain hidden imitations. Intermediate ricercar sections, which are quite common in Venetian toccatas, occur only in three pieces (L15–17); they are based on variants of a single theme, treated in stretto (Ex. 39).

Sweelinck employs various devices to enhance continuity. They include the 'reverberation' of the ricercar theme during the initial bars

Ex. 39

of the subsequent virtuoso section (Ex. 40 (a)); the opposite procedure—that is, with the figuration already beginning during the final cadence of the ricercar (Ex. 40 (b)); and the same device applied to the transition between the opening chordal bars and the toccata proper (Ex. 40 (c)).

Ex. 40

Typical features of Sweelinck's toccata style are fanfare motifs (Ex. 41 (*a*)); intervals, for instance a fifth, presented in various ways (Ex. 41 (*b*)); and melodic elements conflicting with musical metre (Ex. 41 (*c*)). The relationship between consecutive melodic elements is shown in Ex. 42. Motif (*a*), derived from segment 1, reappears coupled with an octave leap (*b*) in segment II; subsequently (*b*), ascending as well as descending, connects the repeats of a new element (*c*) in segment III. In this way Sweelinck assures the coherence of material contained in a non-thematic composition. The macro-structure, which is largely determined by the harmonic rhythm, will be discussed in the last section of this chapter.

Ex. 41

Ex. 42

According to a theory advanced by Murray C. Bradshaw, both the Venetian toccatas and those of Sweelinck are structurally dependent on pre-existing chant material: that is, psalm tones.[12] As these are neither presented in long notes nor otherwise—they only fit the chain of consecutive harmonies—the author speaks of 'ideal cantus firmi'. With the exception of the ricercar sections, occuring in L15–7, the psalm tones, repeated three to thirteen times, cover the entire material of the toccatas in question.

Although this theory should not be dismissed summarily, it meets with serious objections. Leaving aside the Venetians, one wonders why Sweelinck should have made use of chant melodies or, for that matter, of pre-existing tunes at all. Elsewhere, Bradshaw mentions that the composer 'would have had to play [on] every sermon day both [in the] morning and [the] evening "before and after the sermon" and also to play variations on the psalms to be sung by the congregation ... he may have well played his toccatas on the organ as prelude or postlude to the sermon or the service itself ...'.[13] However, there is no evidence for these assertions, let alone proof. And, even if they were true, Sweelinck would have chosen Genevan Calvinist tunes rather than Gregorian psalm tones. Nor are the examples given by Bradshaw convincing. The separate notes of the chant are arbitrarily stretched or shortened, ranging from quavers to ten tied semibreves (a proportion of 1:80!). Unexplained deviations from the psalm tones include repeated mediants and other groups of notes, incomplete or over-complete endings, notes added in square brackets (to fit the composer's harmony), and a final cadence presented twice at the beginning. Obviously, Sweelinck's toccatas serve as Procrustean beds for the chant, whose original configuration has become unrecognizable, even in analysis. In point of fact, using the same licences, it is rather easy to adapt a Genevan psalm tune so that it 'fits' an arbitrarily chosen toccata by Sweelinck. Therefore Bradshaw's theory must be considered untenable.

Curiously enough, none of Sweelinck's German pupils took much interest in the toccata. It was only the generation after them (Weckmann, Reincken, Buxtehude; and, in south Germany, Froberger) which cultivated and developed this keyboard genre. Sweelinck's toccatas are far from negligible, however. They include true master-pieces, such as L15–17 and L24. Unlike Andrea Gabrieli, he did not need thematic material to arrive at a firm construction.

Variation Cycles: Sacred Melodies

The first complete edition of Sweelinck's instrumental music (*Works*, i, 1894) contained only two variation cycles based on sacred tunes. In the volume's revised edition by the same editor, Max Seiffert (1943), this number had increased to twenty-four. Apart from ten authentic works discovered during the period of half a century, the new edition included twelve anonymous cycles attributed to the Amsterdam organist on fairly dubious grounds. One is surprised at Seiffert's inadvertent generosity, the more so as he possessed a thorough knowledge of Sweelinck's keyboard style. Hardly less amazing is the fact that neither Sigtenhorst Meyer (1946), nor Tusler (1958), questioned these attributions. Yet the stylistic features and the technical deficiencies found in several cycles precludes Sweelinck's authorship. Moreover, in some cases undisputable facts would have sufficed to debar a specific work: for instance, the occurrence of b'' in Seiffert's no. 47, a note not included in the compass of either the large or the small organ of the Oude Kerk.

During the 1960s, several scholars, notably Breig and Curtis, purged the 1943 edition, rejecting the twelve anonymous cycles (two of the latter could be assigned to Henderick Speuy and Heinrich Scheidemann respectively). On the other hand, four authentic works had been discovered since the Second World War. As a result, *Opera omnia*, i, Fasc. 2, edited by Alfons Annegarn (1968), contains fourteen sets of variations, a few of which are certainly or probably incomplete. In comparison with the 1943 edition, the higher average quality of this collection is self-evident.

Keyboard settings of sacred tunes were quite common in the sixteenth century, but there can be no doubt that Sweelinck was the first to compose variation cycles on liturgical melodies. As these had no function in the Calvinist service, he must have written them for performance during his daily concerts. Unlike later works of this kind they do not begin with the statement of the theme, which was obviously considered to be known by the audience.[14] The same is true of the composer's secular variation cycles, to be discussed subsequently. The extensive knowledge of the international song repertory by the Dutch public in Sweelinck's time may be explained by the fact that liturgical, semi-liturgical, and even secular melodies were freely exchanged among various confessions; this happened by means of translations or *contrafacta*. Even when they had no place in the official liturgy—as was the case in the Dutch Reformed Church—they were widely used in private devotions.

The usual number of variations in each cycle is four. Exceptions include A3, A7, and A10 (three variations), A12 (five variations), and A5 (six variations); A16* consisting of two bicinia on Psalm 60 is almost certainly incomplete. In general, the number of voices remains constant within the separate variations, but their sequence shows a slight preference for a gradual increase from two to four, sometimes preceded by a four-part setting. *Freistimmigkeit* occurs only exceptionally (for example in A11, variations 3 and 4).

As regards the tunes, the composer's choice reflects the same 'ecumenical' attitude we encountered in his vocal music. They include three Roman chant melodies (one of them better known as a folksong), five items taken from the Dutch Psalter, and six Lutheran chorales. No conclusions can be drawn from the proportions between these categories. As with other genres the number of preserved works—mostly in German sources—form only a minor part of the total output. Among the lost cycles there must have been many based on Genevan psalm tunes.

The compositional technique is that of the cantus firmus variation, the pre-existing melody being presented in one of the parts, either integrally or slightly ornamented, and rhythmically changed. Only in variation 4 of A1 ('Allein Gott in der Höh sei Ehr') does the tune switch during the repeat of the first phrase from the highest to the upper-middle part, the treble remaining silent. In his treatment of the voices set against the cantus firmus Sweelinck brilliantly exploits all the techniques available to him. They include the use of material derived from the tune as anticipatory imitation (often with shortened note values and occasionally inverted); short countersubjects treated in the same way; and figuration in the style of the English virginalists, but more rigidly controlled and sometimes concealing motifs borrowed from the cantus firmus.

Two of the cycles based on chant melodies, the hymn 'Christe qui lux est et dies' (A3) and the antiphon 'Da pacem, Domine, in diebus nostris' (A4), present the cantus firmus in equal note-values without any ornamentation. These tunes, both consisting exclusively of repeated notes, minor and major seconds, and minor thirds, have so shallow a profile that the composer was compelled to use external means (countersubjects, non-thematic figuration, sections in triple time) to achieve the necessary contrast and variety. The Genevan psalms and Lutheran chorales, on the other hand, offer ample opportunity for the elaboration of material derived from the cantus firmus. This does not mean, however, that in these cycles the composer employs the technique of the psalm or chorale ricercar. Within the separate variations both external and internal elements have a share in the astonishingly unpredictable diversity of compositional procedures. Example 43 shows a few fragments taken from variation 3 of 'Allein zu Dir Herr Jesu Christ' (A2). All of them appear in the chorale's first strain and its repeat.

Ex. 43 (*b*) shows the setting of a canonically treated countersubject accompanying the slightly ornamented cantus firmus in the treble. The

Ex. 43

canon is typical of Sweelinck's technique: the middle voice answers the bass first at the upper octave, and then from bar 153 onwards at the upper fourth. Ex. 43 (c) displays an amazing feat of contrapuntal ingenuity. At first sight it seems an unequivocal example of anticipatory imitation by the middle voice, the notes $e'–d'–b–c'$ prefiguring the opening of the cantus firmus's second subphrase (bars 157–8). Strictly speaking, however, this cannot be the case, as the note b does not belong to the original tune (see Ex. 43 (a)). The true configuration of this melodic formula is only found in bars 158–60, and there it appears in a form slightly different as to pitch and intervallic relations: $c''–b'–g'–a'$. So it was not the middle voice but the underlying bass which anticipated the four notes of the cantus firmus, and this was done in proportional acceleration: one minim, two crotchets, and one quaver. Subsequently the roles of the two lower voices are exchanged. Now it is the middle voice which becomes the anticipant, presenting the motif in fourfold diminution, while the bass, proceeding at the lower third, follows it (bar 157). However, when this formula is taken over literally by the upper voice (bar 158), the analyst becomes bewildered. Which is imitating which? Does the cantus firmus imitate the counter-voices? Do the counter-voices, prematurely, imitate the cantus firmus? Does the cantus firmus imitate (anticipate) itself? Whatever the answer may be, it is worthwhile having a look at the cantus firmus itself, leaving aside the lower voices. We find three consecutive variants of the four-note motif: first a version starting on e'', including the non-thematic note b'; then a doubly diminished version resulting from the embellishment of the note c'' (bar 158), and finally the integral configuration in double note values (assuming a 'psychological' duration of a minim of the same c''). In point of fact, the second and third versions together form a miniature mensuration canon within a single voice! Note also the pivotal position of the c'' in bar 158: it functions as the end of the motif's first version as well as the beginning of both the second and third versions. In the meantime, the two lower voices do not remain contrapuntally inactive. Having dealt with the cantus firmus, they now start imitating each other with freely invented motifs. The middle voice in bar 158 is answered by the bass at the lower third (bar 159), and the same happens with a descending scale spanning an octave, this time in stretto and at the interval of a fifth (bars 159–60). The concluding three bars (162–4) contain a 'walking' bass. It is characteristic of the Amsterdam composer that even this *fondamento* passage derives from previous material (see the middle voice in bar 161). The description of the procedures shown in Ex. 43 (*c*) has now taken us about a page; Sweelinck, on the other hand, needed only nine bars.

Next, the chorale's first phrase is repeated. Although the settings of both the antecedent and the consequent are less intricate than those of the first statement, they strongly enhance the diversity within the variation as a whole. Ex. 43 (*d*) shows a toccata-like treatment of the bass, whose figuration starts with a motif taken from the middle voice and imitated at the lower octave. The second subphrase (Ex. 43 (*e*)) is anticipated by the middle voice in halved note values, homophonically supported by the bass, which subsequently evolves as a free counter-voice. But here again, freedom is subject to planning and control; during the whole subphrase the rhythm gradually accelerates: crotchets, quavers, semiquavers.

The remaining phrases of the tune are treated in the same manner, displaying a kaleidoscopic diversity of techniques. It was undoubtedly this multiform aspect of the composer's procedures which induced previous authors to speak of whimsicality and lack of coherence. A comparison with the fantasias not only shows the untenability of these statements, but also sheds light on the unity of Sweelinck's instrumental output. If we take the cantus firmus as the *analogon* of the fantasia's theme, then the treatment of the counter-voices in both genres (whether derived from the theme or contrasting with it) shows a remarkable procedural affinity. In fact, it is possible both to regard a variation cycle as a fantasia based on a pre-existing theme, *and* to consider a single variation as a micro-fantasia.

Although in general the cantus firmus remains clearly recognizable during the whole set, some cycles include variations presenting the tune completely dissolved in figuration. Variation 6 of A5 ('Erbarme Dich mein, o Herre Gott') offers an example of this kind of mini-toccata (Ex. 44).

Finally, a remark should be made about the cycle on 'Ons is gheboren een kindekijn' (A8). This melody, originally a *Benedicamus Domino* to which the text 'Puer nobis nascitur' was sung as a prosula, eventually became a Dutch folksong. The style of Sweelinck's setting considerably differs from that of the other cycles. It is above all the dance-like character of the melody which gives the impression of a secular set of variations. In point of fact, only the origin of the tune justifies its inclusion in the collection of sacred works. Here we find no learned procedures; but it is precisely the disarming simplicity of the setting which contributes to its undeniable charm.

Apart from the fantasias, no other form of keyboard music cultivated by Sweelinck proved as influential as the sacred variation cycles. His pupils Scheidt and Scheidemann both excelled in it.

Variations on Secular Tunes

As one would expect, most of the compositional procedures found in the sacred cycles are also encountered in the works based on secular melodies. Only the consistently applied cantus firmus technique is absent from the latter category. However, though the same devices occur in both subgenres, the practice of the application is different. The reason for this lies in a number of opposing characteristics inherent in the two types of melody, shown in Table 2:

Ex. 44

cantus firmus

TABLE 2

Sacred melody	Secular melody
origin: chant or old song	origin: modern song or dance
modal	tonal
self-supporting	dependent on harmony
small compass	large compass
free rhythm, unprofiled with only two different note values	rhythm subject to musical metre, sharply profiled with four to six different note values
free periodic phrases	regular periodic phrases
phrases not repeated (except the first in some chorales)	first phrase always repeated; other phrases suitable for repeat

Admittedly this antithetical image is somewhat overstated. The secular melodies especially do not always answer to each of these criteria. Yet, in general, the respective characteristics strongly determine the application of different variation techniques. This is also true of works belonging to the same category but based on contrasting types of melody. A comparison of two secular cycles, 'Est-ce Mars' (N3) and 'Ick voer al over Rhijn' (N4), may elucidate the latter point. The French *air de cour* (Ex. 45 (*a*)), having a range of a tenth, is sharply profiled in two unequal phrases, one of four, the other of five bars. The Dutch folksong (Ex. 45 (*b*)), on the other hand, consists exclusively of steps of seconds (except the initial upbeat); its rhythm lacks inner contrasts and its range covers only a sixth. The two phrases, each of seven bars, are symmetrical. As a result of the opposite characters of the two themes, the variation techniques used by Sweelinck are also antithetical. The possibilities contained in the French melody are so rich that the composer needed hardly any

Ex. 45

111

external material. The only countermotifs (marked here with crosses) appear at the opening of variation 5 (Ex. 46); otherwise, the theme itself suffices for the display of contrapuntal virtuosity (Ex. 47).

In the other cycle the theme is provided with a great number of

Ex. 46

Ex. 47

countersubjects and motifs, most of which are consistently elaborated, for instance by inversion (Ex. 48 (*a*)) or proportional acceleration (Ex. 48 (*b*) and (*c*)). Continuity between the phrases is enhanced by a special device, which is also occasionally applied in the sacred cycles (for example in A11, bars 32 ff.). The last note of a variation or a phrase does not end on a bare chord, but its final bar is instead filled up with a graceful ornamental turn. While Sweelinck borrowed this device from the Elizabethan and Jacobean virginalists, he carried it further. The same motif reappears in the next phrase and there it adopts quite a different function, namely that of a countersubject to the theme (Ex. 48 (*d*)).

Ex. 48

Despite their differences, the two cycles also include common elements such as variations in toccata style (N3, variation 4; N4, variations 3 and 4) and variations in triple time (as N4 is already in 3/2, this becomes 9/4). Both works represent the peak of the genre, and the same is true of a few other cycles: 'Mein junges Leben hat ein End' (N6), 'Onder een linde groen' (N8), and the student song 'More palatino' (N7).

The settings of dances, on the other hand, are uneven in quality. An excellent piece is the parody of Peter Philip's Pavan (N11). It shows Sweelinck's supreme art of transforming an existing composition into a creation of his own, comparable to the reworking of Italian madrigals included in the *Rimes* of 1612 (see pp. 41–3). There is no justification, however, for playing down the quality of Philip's youthful composition (1580) in favour of the Amsterdam master, as was done by Sigtenhorst Meyer.[15] The original English work and the Dutch restatement are fashioned in different styles. Philips writes idiomatically for the virginal; his melody receives a *freistimmig* chordal support. Sweelinck, on the other hand, reshapes the piece into a strict four-part contrapuntal setting, and his figuration shows the consistency and control typical of his other works. As a result, his version is not only well suited to the virginal or harpsichord, but also to the organ. The same cannot be said of Philips's piece.

The other stylized pavan restated by Sweelinck is Dowland's famous *Pavana Lachrymae* (N10). The only source of this work—the Bártfa tablature, compiled and transcribed by the rather obscure Slovak organist Zacharias Zarewutius—is far from trustworthy. Although the corrupt reading, transmitted to us in a manuscript dating from at least forty years after Sweelinck's death, precludes a comparison with Dowland's composition, the Dutchman's 'coloured' version does not match his reworking of the *Pavana Philippi*.

Among the less distinguished works there is also a small set based on the *Pavana hispanica* (N9). This cycle of four variations, preserved in two different sources together with variations on the same tune by Samuel Scheidt, has for some time been a matter of controversy. The idea of master and pupil having collaborated, advanced by Seiffert and refuted by Sigtenhorst Meyer, is today no longer accepted. However, the biographer's assertion that Sweelinck's fourth variation in triple time cannot have been the last, is untenable.[16] The prolongation of the final chord with an additional bar clearly points to the cycle's conclusion.

Another case is the set of five variations on the *Ballo del Granduca*

(N1) which, like the restatement of Dowland's *Pavana Lachrymae*, is preserved only in the Bártfa tablature. This is a work of great charm, but is it really by Sweelinck? In 1968, I included it without hesitation in the canon of authentic compositions, but since then some doubts have arisen. The absence of contrapuntal variations is in itself no reason to question its authenticity, but the lack of variety within the separate items is certainly atypical. If, nevertheless, this cycle is Sweelinck's work, then it must have been written for pedagogical purposes. Each variation presents a specific difficulty such as passage-work in the right hand (variation 2); a 'walking' bass (variation 3); figuration in semiquavers (variation 4); and the doubling of the melody in thirds and sixths (variation 5).

For some reason, the eight variations on the *Poolsche dans* (N12) have always been tacitly undervalued. Yet this is a splendid work, showing a rich display of different compositional techniques. The theme (Ex. 49 (*a*)) does not disclaim its dance origins, but in the course of the variations it adopts more and more the character of an 'abstract' melody, because of its subjection to various contrapuntal de.ices. In variation 2, the opening notes are joined by a countersubject presenting a variant of the theme in fourfold diminution, both literal and by inversion (Ex. 49 (*b*)). The theme's rhythmical transformation in variation 3 affects its character, and the restatement presents a new melodic version, which is subsequently twice carried through all the voices (Ex. 49 (*c*)). After a brilliant display of figuration against the tune in the treble (variation 4), the latter appears in the bass, joined by a chromatic countersubject that is presented four times, the last time in augmentation (variation 5; Ex. 49 (*d*)). There follows without a break, a variation in triple time, thematic figuration in the upper voice alternating with non-thematic figuration in the bass. In the penultimate variation this technique is maintained, each of the two phrases appearing first integrally and then resolved in semiquavers. Finally, the eighth variation presents the theme throughout in the tenor, a device probably borrowed from William Byrd; it is also found in the last variation of N3. As in 'Ick voer al over Rhijn', the cycle ends with a coda in which a motif derived from the tune's second phrase functions as an 'echo' (Ex. 49 (*e*)).

Nowhere in Sweelinck's instrumental music is the English influence so easily demonstrable as in the settings of secular songs and dances. As was shown by Curtis, the figuration patterns are (or at least seem to have been) derived from contemporary composers such as Farnaby, Byrd, and Bull, as well as from older masters (Tallis and Blitheman).

116

Ex. 49

The way in which the Dutchman became acquainted with their works cannot be established unequivocally, but he certainly saw Peter Philips again in Antwerp (1604), and may have received a visit from John Bull in 1617, when the latter acted as a consultant for the building of a new organ in St John's Cathedral of Bois-le-Duc ('s-Hertogenbosch). At any rate, the cultural contacts between the Republic and England were so close and frequent that it must have been rather easy for the Amsterdam organist to become familiar with the music of his contemporaries on the other side of the North Sea.

Today the settings of secular tunes are the best-known pieces among Sweelinck's keyboard works. Less austere than the fantasias and sacred cycles, and offering more variety, they seem to attract the amateur harpsichordist. This collection of twelve works is particularly well suited to be an introduction to Sweelinck's instrumental music in general.

Lute Music

Sweelinck's pieces for the lute must be understood as products of his leisure hours. They were probably played within the circle of his family or during informal gatherings with his friends. There is no evidence that the Amsterdam organist was a virtuoso on the lute, but being an all-round musician, he may have had a fairly good command of the most popular instrument of his time. Only seven pieces have survived. Four of them, three voltas and one courante, are included in the Lute-Book of Edward Herbert, Lord of Cherbury, who visited the Republic twice between 1608 and 1617. Two of the voltas are provided with *doubles* (N19 and N20). A few imitated motifs betray the contrapuntist, but for the rest these simple dances offer no more than pleasant music. The most attractive piece among them is the courante (N17).

Three Genevan psalm settings included in the lengthy Thysius Manuscript are of a higher quality. The sacred tunes are abundantly ornamented; imitations of short motifs (sometimes anticipatory) appear in the middle voices and the bass. A comparison with the keyboard cycles, based on Genevan psalms (A10–12 and A16), reveals some affinity as regards the imitative treatment of floridly diminished notes. Yet there is no trace of cantus firmus technique which, for that matter, would have been difficult to realize on the lute. More appropriate is a confrontation with the psalm settings for keyboard in the Susanne van Soldt Manuscript, compiled during the 1570s.[17] It sheds light on Sweelinck's expert coloration technique. Two corresponding passages from Psalm 23 are reproduced in Ex. 50.[18]

Ex. 50

Susanne van Soldt Ms, no. 8

Sweelinck (N16)

Although Sweelinck's lute pieces do not reveal his genius, these works, unconnected with his professional activities, form an interesting marginal aspect of his art.

Forma Formans[19]

In Sweelinck's time, the concept of music still denoted an activity rather than an object. This, perhaps, gives us a clue about how to resolve the problem raised by traditional analysis: is the composer a master of exquisite details, capriciously connected in a loose overall form, or is he a cerebral architect whose creations are conceived mathematically? To find the answer, it is necessary to abandon traditional methods of analysis and concentrate on the compositional activity instead of the completed piece of music. We must study factors rather than elements. In other words, it is the *forma formans*, the form forming itself, rather than the *forma formata*, the formed form, which may reveal the truth.

The following hypothesis serves as a starting-point. In Sweelinck's instrumental music, structural factors come across as movement. They are time factors, affecting our experience of time. They cause psychic deviations from the clock time and may therefore be viewed as categories of tension.

Thus the number of basic structural factors is limited to three: acceleration, retardation, and stabilization. With Sweelinck, every kind of acceleration or retardation is proportional and can consequently be expressed in numbers. If the acceleration or retardation concerns the melody, one usually employs the spatial terms diminution and augmentation. Gradual acceleration or retardation of tempo (accelerando or ritardando) occurred only very rarely in Sweelinck's time and was certainly never prescribed. However, acceleration was employed by distinct gradations, a procedure which I shall indicate by the word 'stretto'. It should be observed that in forma formans, this term embraces much more than the familiar stretto device in a fantasia or a fugue. It denotes all types of gradated acceleration.

Let us now look at the short set of variations on the *Engelsche Fortuyn* (N2), the melody of which is given in Ex. 51 (*a*). In the four-part opening variation the melody is treated as a series of short canons between the two upper voices. The lower voices have a merely harmonic function, which does not preclude them from proceeding parallel to one of the canonic parts from time to time. As a whole, this first variation gives the impression of repose. There is no tension

between the tune and the borrowed material. If we look at the score, this lack of tension is maintained during the second variation; it seems as if the overall image is even more balanced here than in the first, which contained more ornamental passages. Yet on reflection it becomes clear that in the second variation, the tension has increased. The most conspicuous motif of the melody, the descending tetrachord, is repeated in halved note values by the lower voices (Ex. 51 (*b*)) and, besides, incorporated in the figuration (Ex. 51 (*c*)). Moreover, this figuration also includes a motif which reduces the first phrase to its essence (Ex. 51 (*d*)). The same devices are applied to the third variation, except that there the borrowed material is first reduced to one half of its value, then to one fourth (Ex. 51 (*e*)), and finally to one half again. These accelerated fragments do not only appear in the lower voices, they are likewise adopted by the treble which, though ornamented, constantly reproduces the melody in its initial motion. As a matter of fact, Ex. 51 (*e*) is taken from the treble.

Exactly what has happened now? Three times we have heard the complete tune in the upper voice, with figurations indeed, but nevertheless in unchanging movement. However, the material borrowed from the tune was presented in a stepwise acceleration. In the first variation the ratio of motion between the tune and derived material is 1:1; in the second variation it is 1:2; and in the final variation it is augmented to 1:4. In the course of the work, two different factors of motion appear simultaneously, one constant and the other accelerated by stages. Therefore, the overall structure of this set of variations may be described as a stretto.

A still more refined and compressed application of the same structural device is encountered in the cycle based on the Lutheran chorale 'Ich ruf zu Dir, Herr Jesu Christ' (A6; see Ex. 52). In this instance, the whole process of acceleration is enacted within the framework of a single variation, the first of the set. This variation is a bicinium. The upper voice presents the liturgical melody almost integrally, while the lower voice borrows from this melody a number of fragments, which either anticipate or imitate the cantus firmus. As in the *Engelsche Fortuyn* variations, the note values of the borrowed material are gradually reduced, but in addition, Sweelinck adds to the chain of reductions a number of intermediate links. The gaps between the proportions are bridged by fragments which somewhere in the middle move into double speed (See Ex. 52 (*a*) and (*c*)). Such a link in the chain constitutes, not only in relation to the cantus firmus, but also in relation to itself, a gradual acceleration. It may therefore be considered a micro-stretto.

Briefly, the structural course is the following. The lower part exposes the opening phrase of the chorale, first as a literal anticipation, but after two bars in double speed. The latter proportion between the two voices is stabilized in the second fragment. Now the same device is applied to the third and fourth, as well as the fifth and sixth fragments: that is, the note values are gradually reduced. The structural image becomes clearer if one expresses the growing tension between the unchanging motion of the treble and the accelerating motion of the lower voice in numbers. The first fragment is a micro-stretto proceeding from 1:1 to 1:2; the second fragment, a confirmation of the ration 1:2; the third fragment, a stretto from 1:2 to 1:4; the fourth

Ex. 52

fragment, a confirmation of 1:4; the fifth fragment, a rhythmical link between 1:4 and 1:8, and the last fragment, a confirmation of 1:8.

As a whole, the variation is structured as a macro-stretto in which, through the insertion of a number of micro-strettos, the tension between the two simultaneous categories of motion grows in a particularly smooth way. As in the cycle on the *Engelsche Fortuyn*, the visual image of the score hardly reveals anything of this factor of tension. The borrowed material in the lower voice is completely integrated into the figuration, and this figuration gives the impression of whimsicality rather than a steady growth towards a climax. But it has now become evident that the apparent lack of coherence in Sweelinck's compositional technique is deceptive. Actually, this technique shows quite a calculated handling of factors of motion.

In both works discussed so far, tension became increased by a gradual reduction of the *melodic* rhythm. It goes without saying that strict application of this device to a composition without proper themes—for instance, a toccata—is virtually impossible. But the possibilities of musical rhythm are not restricted to the succession of pitches only. The succession of harmonies also possesses its rhythm and it is this harmonic rhythm which Sweelinck handles as the most important factor of motion in his toccatas. As an example I have taken his best-known work in this genre, the toccata L16. Here we encounter (after the introductory and ricercar sections) a number of harmonic progressions, each of which shows a gradual acceleration of the harmonic rhythm (see Table 3).

TABLE 3
Harmonic Rhythm in Toccata L16

Series	Bars	Rhythmical course (bars)
1	44–55	4–2–2–2–2
2	56–80	4–5–2–2–2–2–1–1–1–1–1–2–¾–¼
3	81–94	2–1–2–1–1–½–½–1–¼–¼–¼–¼–¼–¼–½–½–½–½–1–½
4	95–106	3–1½–½–½–½–½–½–½–½–1–1–½–½–½–½
5	107–22	2–1–1–1–2–¾–¼–¼–¼–¼–¼–¼–¼–¼–¼–½–½–½–½–½–½–½–½–½–½–½
6	123–38	1½–½–2–3–3–3–3

The first progression starts with a harmonic duration of four bars, followed by four units of two bars each. The second begins even more slowly—a group of four bars is followed by one of five—but then the motion gradually accelerates, and the progression closes with units of approximately one bar. The pattern of the subsequent progressions is virtually the same: each time the harmonic rhythm is subjected to an acceleration process. Only the sixth and last progression reveals the opposite tendency: a gradual slowing down till the end of the piece.

It is not easy to establish strict norms for the evaluation of a harmonic succession, as the degree of tension between two consecutive chords is not always the same. For example, a chord of the fourth degree in root position, which is followed by the first inversion of the triad on the second degree, does not really influence the harmonic course. I have therefore eliminated a number of secondary chordal connections, in which the bass remains unchanged. Further, it is true that within the individual series the rhythm sometimes fluctuates. There is no question of absolute regularity. Nevertheless, the overall image of harmonic rhythm in this toccata is clearly analogous to the melodic rhythm in the variation cycles discussed above. Significantly, the harmonic progressions do not always proceed in phase with the sections of the composition. Each of them is an autonomous micro-stretto and, with the exception of the last one, they form together a macro-stretto.

These three examples do not exhaust the stock of Sweelinck's stretto devices. The composer also applies the principle of acceleration in other ways, of which I will mention only a few. Acceleration of what could be called canonic rhythm is best explained by an example. The second variation of the cycle based on the song 'Onder een linde groen' (N8) starts with a series of short canons, the melodic material of which is derived from the tune. In the first canon the lower voice answers at the distance of a semibreve, in the second after a minim, in the third after a crotchet, and finally both voices run simultaneously, that is, as a *canon sine pausis*. Since each canon is already by definition a stretto, one could speak, in this case too, of four micro-strettos forming together a macro-stretto (Ex. 53).

In principle, it is not necessary that factors of acceleration should always be conditioned by rhythm. When a melodic unit becomes contracted, that is, gradually deprived of 'superfluous' notes, leaving at the end only a small motif, then we can speak of a non-rhythmic, purely melodic, stretto. Sweelinck employs this device mostly in his toccatas and echo fantasias (Ex. 54). Sometimes this melodic stretto is ingeniously combined with the gradual acceleration of the canonic rhythm (Ex. 55).

In addition, we find numerous examples of apparent acceleration, an effect that results from the diminution of a melodic unit. Although the movement remains stable, the padding of the melodic skeleton with

Ex. 53

Ex. 54

Toccata L17

Ex. 55

Echo fantasia L14

127

quavers and semiquavers gives the impression of rhythmic quickening. One hardly notices the exact moment when the melody proper ends and free figuration begins.

Against all these acceleration devices, there are few examples of proportional retardation. If the composer adopts a much slower tempo, this happens mostly in a rather abrupt way at the beginning of a new melodic or harmonic series. The rare instances of gradual stretching of a melodic unit, occurring for instance in the Chromatic Fantasia (L1; bars 140–4), are caused by retardation of the harmonic rhythm. It seems that in such a case, the melodic slowing down is dictated by the harmonic motion. However, retardation and acceleration sometimes occur simultaneously, as when a gradually subsiding harmonic rhythm is combined with gradual acceleration of the melody. These two structural factors are opposed; nevertheless, they do not neutralize each other, being too dissimilar. Each of them retains his autonomous function, and together they suggest quietude as well as animation.

Finally, a few words should be said about the third fundamental factor of structure, that of stabilization. When a degree of tension has been reached, it is often maintained for a considerable time. It is during these stable episodes that the composer makes use of a spatial device, the echo. As a means of musical expression the echo is determined by space, and for Sweelinck this aspect is obviously of more interest than the original Arcadian connotation. Spatial suggestion as a factor of stabilization is mostly encountered when a melodic entity is presented in slow motion. If this melody lies in the bass, it will dictate a very slow harmonic rhythm. A characteristic example, already discussed previously, is found in the fantasia L2 (see the section entitled *The Fantasias*, earlier in this chapter). Here the principal theme is played in fourfold augmentation by the pedal, accompanied with small echo motifs by the manuals.

What conclusions can be drawn from the investigation of forma formans in Sweelinck's works? In the first place, the lack of coherence, proclaimed by Apel and Tusler, has been disproved. This evaluation was based on criteria of form and did not consider the structure. Moreover, it seems that these writers used late baroque standards for their judgements. If Sweelinck's compositional technique conforms to an aesthetic principle, then this should not be sought in the second half of the seventeenth century or even later, but in his own time and the century before him, that is, the Renaissance. Sweelinck's so-called whimsicality is nothing but a very personal, perhaps mannerist, application of the old precept of *varietas*.

This concept was derived from classical rhetoric and plays an important role in Renaissance aesthetics. In his treatise on the art of painting (*De pictura*), which dates from 1436, Leon Battista Alberti speaks about the importance of *copia* and *varietas* (abundance and variety) in a narrative painting; he also points to the necessity of variety in the arts of cooking and music.[20] That this concept was retained is indicated in a work by Carel van Mander, a Dutch contemporary of Sweelinck. In his *Book of Painting* he refers to Alberti's emphasis on the importance of variety.[21] Not only in writings on the visual arts, but also in those on music, was variety as an aesthetic concept amply discussed. Johannes Tinctoris devoted a whole chapter of his *Liber de arte contrapuncti* to this subject. He refers to the *Poetics* of Horace and the *Rhetorics* of Cicero, and explicitly prescribes the use of variety in all aspects of musical composition.[22]

It goes without saying that the aesthetic principle of variety is the basis of music of all times and places. But this does not imply that all composers have interpreted and realized this idea in the same way. Sweelinck applies the precept by presenting a great variety of rhythmically contrasting motifs within a brief space of time. The generations who came after him brought more 'regularity' to their musical textures, causing less frequent contrasts. The compositions of Sweelinck's pupil, Heinrich Scheidemann, already give an image which seems much more quiet than that of his teacher's works. When, at the end of the seventeenth century, Corelli established the norms of sonata and concerto, his kind of *varietas* differed essentially from that of Sweelinck. If we listen with anachronistic ears, it seems that the Amsterdam composer indulges every arbitrary thought and loses all traces of the main lines.

But we know now that at the root of the seemingly gratuitous and disorderly interplay of contrasting motifs there lies a control of factors of motion determining the inner organization. These factors connect heterogenous elements and give the work a unity which we perceive while listening, but which seemed to be lacking when the forma formata was analysed. And so the study of forma formans has provided us with the answer to the question raised previously: Sweelinck is a master both of exquisite detail and firmly organized structure.

V
CONCLUSION

Since the beginning of the twentieth century, Sweelinck's legacy to the German school of organists has been amply discussed, so little need be said here about this subject. The composer's influence spread over the entire German territory, not to mention Denmark, Sweden, and Poland. It lasted until the 1660s and is especially demonstrable in the organ works of Samuel Scheidt and Heinrich Scheidemann. In addition, Scheidt's *Cantiones sacrae* of 1620 clearly show the influence of Sweelinck's vocal style; the same can be said for the psalm and chorale settings of other pupils. In Hamburg, the Amsterdam master was nicknamed 'the organist maker', the posts at the three main churches of that city being occupied for a long time by Praetorius, Scheidemann, and Cernitz. The first two transmitted Sweelinck's heritage to their gifted pupils Matthias Weckmann and Jan Adam Reincken respectively. A particularly brilliant organist, Reincken seems to have played Sweelinck's works continuously during his long life (1623–1722); so it is quite possible that the young Bach, who visited Hamburg to hear the aged Reincken playing on the splendid organ of St Catherine's Church, became acquainted with Sweelinck's music. Yet the influence of the Dutch composer on the German organ school of the late seventeenth and early eighteenth centuries should not be exaggerated (as was done by Seiffert). Sweelinck's name was certainly still known at that time; however, considerable stylistic changes had occurred over the previous eighty years: textures had adopted a 'classical' simplicity, and tonality had gained mastery over formal arrangements. Whereas the survival of Sweelinck's art in late baroque music in general cannot be demonstrated, his fugal procedures were certainly transmitted in the course of the century.

Less is known about the composer's influence in his own country, since very little music has been preserved. Dirck Sweelinck faithfully followed his father's path. Of his works, only a few vocal pieces survive, including the masterly five-part *Cecilia-Liedt*, which could easily pass for a chanson of Jan Pieterszoon, were it not set to Dutch words. If Dirck is the composer of the beautiful keyboard cycle on the chorale

'Wie schön leuchtet der Morgenstern' (preserved anonymously in a south German manuscript), this would provide further evidence for his adherence to the style of his father. According to a remark by Anthoni van Noordt (in the dedication of his *Tabulatuur-Boeck* to the burgomasters of Amsterdam, in 1659), many Dutch organists composed instrumental psalm settings, undoubtedly to be played during their daily concerts. As for van Noordt himself, he was a formidable contrapuntist; despite the more 'classical' style of his psalms and fantasias, his debt to Sweelinck is undeniable.[1]

Sweelinck's influence on Dutch vocal music is more difficult to trace. The most outstanding composer during the first half of the century was Jan Baptist Verrijt (d. 1650), whose recently discovered *Flammae divinae* (motets and Masses for two and three parts) offer a splendid synthesis of traditional Netherlands polyphony and modern *stile concertato*.[2] Verrijt probably knew Sweelinck's motets of 1619, if not the Psalter; however, a direct influence of these works cannot be established.

As it is risky to attempt a brief description of Sweelinck's greatness, I shall abstain from doing so. Two concluding observations should be made, however. The first regards the unity of the composer's output. While it is true that, from a historical point of view, his vocal music marks the end of an era, and the instrumental works the inauguration of a new epoch, this should not be taken as an evaluation, nor does it point to a compositional dichotomy between the two fields of production. Apart from individual traits, such as vocal text interpretation and instrumental figurative writing, Sweelinck's works in both categories have much in common. Contrapuntal procedures present in the chansons, psalms, and motets are also encountered in the fantasias and variation cycles; the same is true of cantus firmus settings and even the antiphonal treatment of voices. Whether Sweelinck wrote vocal or instrumental music, his composition technique remained virtually unchanged.

Second, Sweelinck is a truly Dutch composer. Despite the fact that he left not a single work set to words in his native language, his compositions reflect the character of the Dutch people in general. The renunciation of spectacular dramatic effects and stunningly monumental splendour in favour of a loving cultivation of detail, picturesque representation and mathematically contrived balance is characteristic of Dutch painting, poetry, and music alike. Even when Sweelinck, exceptionally, tackled music of larger dimensions (as in Book III of the

131

Psalms), he never betrayed the intimacy of his art. His genius does not reveal itself spontaneously; it is disclosed only by dint of insight and knowledge.

NOTES

CHAPTER I

1. See F. R. Noske, 'Music and Urban Magistrate in 17th-Century Holland', in D. Heartz and B. Wade (edd.) *Report of the Twelfth Congress, Berkeley 1977* (International Musicological Society), (Kassel, 1981), 304–6; and F. R. Noske, *Music Bridging Divided Religions: The Motet in Seventeenth-Century Holland* (Wilhelmshaven, 1988), ch. 1.
2. Original Dutch text in B. van den Sigtenhorst Meyer, *Jan P. Sweelinck en zijn instrumentale muziek* (2nd rev. edn., The Hague, 1946), 28, and R. Tollefsen, 'Jan Petersz. Sweelinck: A Bio-Bibliography', *Tijdschrift van de Vereniging voor Nederlandse Musickgeschiedenis*, 22/2, p. 99. The latter also quotes on the same page a passage from Revius's *History of Deventer* in which the composer is called 'Ioannes Petri Swellingus Daventriensis'.
3. There are no fewer than 25 different spellings known of the name (see Sigtenhorst Meyer, *Jan P. Sweelinck en zijn instrumentale muziek*, p. 269). The composer used only three of these; in chronological order: Swelingh, Swelinck, and Sweelinck.
4. A. Curtis, *Sweelinck's Keyboard Music: A Study of English Elements in Seventeenth-Century Dutch Composition* (Leiden and London, 1969).
5. Only 50 four-part psalms were printed (Düsseldorf, 1568) and reissued in a modern edition of M. Seiffert (Amsterdam, 1899).
6. I cannot share Tollefsen's (implicit) doubts about the currently adopted meaning of the word *psaltes* in Plemp's text. In classical Latin *psaltes* denotes not merely a player of the Greek cithara but in addition a singer or a musician in general. The term is used in the latter sense by several writers including Quintilian and Martianus Capella. As Plemp speaks about Sweelinck in the context of his description of the Oude Kerk, there can be no doubt that in this case *psaltes* should be read as 'organist' (see Tollefsen, 'Jan Pietersz. Sweelinck: A Bio-Bibliography', p. 94).
7. See *The New Grove*, xviii, 412.
8. This is the title of the reprint (*Premier livre des pseaumes de David*) which appeared in 1624. The original edition was entitled *Cinquante pseaumes de David* which suggests that in 1604 Sweelinck was not yet sure whether he would be able to set the complete Psalter.
9. The title quoted by Albert Göhler in his *Verzeichnis der in den Frankfurter und Leipziger Messkatalogen der Jahre 1564 bis 1759 angezeigten Musikalien* (Leipzig, 1902) reads: 'Tabulatura. Fantasien mit 3 Stimmen durch alle 8 Tonos von J.P.S., Organisten zu Amsterdam, komponirt, und von

Samuele Scheid Hallense kolligirt. Fol.; Halle, Melchior Oelschlegel 1630'. The latter year refers to the announcement of the work's publication. Therefore we cannot even be sure whether it ever appeared.

10. Sigtenhorst Meyer, *Jan P. Sweelinck en zijn instrumentale muziek*, p. 69.

11. My previous scepticism about Sweelinck's association with this collection, expressed in my edition of the composer's 'secular' instrumental works (*Opera omnia*, i, Fasc. 3, p. xii), is no longer tenable. Tollefsen lists four different bibliographical references, all with Sweelinck's name and ranging from 1602 to 1759. Only in the last-named year is the book identified by what seems to be its full title: *Nieuw chyter-boek, genaemt Den corten wegwijser die 't hert verheugt* (New Cittern Book, entitled: The Short Guide that Delights the Heart). This indicates an elementary primer for the instrument. See Tollefsen, 'Jan Pietersz. Sweelinck: A Bio-Biography', pp. 96, 98, and 109.

12. G. Baudartius, *Memoryen*, ii. *1620–1624* (Arnhem, 1625), 163. The 'Latin poet' is Horace. Concerning the May song, see F. R. Noske, 'John Bull's Dutch Carol', *Music and Letters*, 46 (1963), 326–33.

13. Plemp states in one of his poems that Sweelinck was not only famous in England and Germany but also in Italy (*Tabellae*, no. xxvii entitled 'Svelingius'). See Tollefsen, 'Jan Pietersz. Sweelinck: A Bio-Biography', p. 93.

CHAPTER II

1. In Jacob Vredeman's five-part setting (*Musica miscella*, Franeker, 1602) the cantus firmus is presented in inversion, a procedure announced by a shallow rhyme in the quinto partbook. Unlike Sweelinck, the composer makes hardly any effort to derive the musical material of the other parts from Lupi's tenor.

2. The word should be read in the old sense of 'mental anguish'.

3. B. van der Sigtenhorst Meyer, *De vocale muzick van Jan P. Sweelinck* (The Hague, 1948), 24.

4. Ibid., pp. 14–16, 55, and 119.

5. I am indebted to Dr James Chater, who kindly provided this information.

6. 'Liquide perle Amor' is included in A. Einstein (ed.) *Luca Marenzio: Sämtliche Werke*, (in Publikationen älterer Musik 4/1, Leipzig, 1929); 'Qual vive Salamandra' in B. Meier and R. Jackson (edd.), *Luca Marenzio: Opera omnia*, 4, (Rome, 1979); 'Io mi son giovinetta' in A. Einstein, *The Italian Madrigal*, 3 (Princeton, 1949); and 'Dolcissimo ben mio' in *Andrea Gabrieli: Complete Madrigals*, 9, (Recent Researches in the Music of the Renaissance xlix), (Madison, 1983).

CHAPTER III

1. P. Pidoux, *Le Psautier huguenot*, (Basle, 1962).
2. G. Voetius, *Politica ecclesiastica*, i. 536 (Amsterdam, 1663).
3. This introductory section owes much to Howard Slenk's excellent article 'Psalms, metrical (the European continent)' in *The New Grove*, xv, 348.
4. The term 'verse' does not refer to the Scriptures; instead, it should be read here as 'stanza'.
5. B. van der Sigtenhorst Meyer, *De vocale muziek van Jan P. Sweelinck* (The Hague, 1948), 115.
6. Ibid., pp. 47, 48, and 148.
7. Ibid., p. 158.
8. Regarding the Lutheran liturgy, see the chorale variations discussed in Chapter IV.
9. Sigtenhorst Meyer, *De vocale muziek van Jan P. Sweelinck*, pp. 152 and 174.
10. Apart from the dissonances, 'crucem' is also depicted through eye-music, the semibreves set to this word being sharpened in four of the five parts. It should be observed that the Dutch term for a sharp, including today's natural, was *cruys* (cross).
11. G. Reese, *Music in the Renaissance*, (rev. edn., New York, 1959), 518.

CHAPTER IV

1. A. Curtis, *Sweelinck's Keyboard Music: A Study of English Elements in Seventeenth-Century Dutch Composition* (Leiden and London, 1969). 163–200. See also *The New Grove*, xiii, 739, Table 7.
2. M. A. Vente, *Die Brabanter Orgel* (Amsterdam, 1963), 267; and H. Klotz, 'Sweelinck spielt Sweelinck', *Beiträge zur Rheinischen Musikgeschichte*, 36 (1961), 37.
3. Curtis, *Sweelinck's Keyboard Music*, pp. 36–44.
4. Sigtenhorst Meyer, *Jan P. Sweelinck en zijn instrumentale muziek* (2nd rev. edn., The Hague, 1946), 164–5.
5. C. van der Borren, *Les origines de la musique de clavier dans les Pays-Bas (Nord et Sud) jusque vers 1630* (Brussels, 1914), 148; for Pirro see *Encyclopédie Lavignac* ii, 2e partie, 1249.
6. W. Apel, *Geschichte der Orgel- und Klaviermusik bis 1700* (Kassel-Basle, 1967), 319–22; see also New Oxford History of Music iv: *The Age of Humanism 1540–1630*, (London, 1968), 635–41, and R. L. Tusler, *The Organ Music of Jan Pieterszoon Sweelinck* (Bilthoven, 1958), 86.
7. Instrumental compositions are identified by their numbering in *Opera omnia*, i, Fasc. 1–3, and preceded by the initials of the respective editors, Leonhardt, Annegarn, and Noske.
8. In 1617 Bull was asked to act as an assessor for the proposed new organ to

be built in St John's Cathedral, 's-Hertogenbosch (Bois-le-Duc). Characteristically, he recommended the extension of the compass of the keyboards to four octaves ($C–c'''$) comprising all the semitones (29 white and 20 black keys).

9. In the manuscript Ly A1 (Berlin, Deutsche Staatsbibliothek), the unique source for this piece, there are only two entries on g'' in the treble instead of the expected three. However, the editor Gustav Leonhardt points to the possibility of six bars having been omitted by the scribe (see the footnote on p. 63 of *Opera omnia*, i, Fasc. 1).

10. See *Opera omnia*, i, Fasc. 1, p. liv.

11. See Johann Mattheson, *Der vollkommene Capellmeister* (Hamburg, 1739), (facs. reprint, Kassel-Basle, 1954), 466.

12. See M. C. Bradhsaw, 'The Toccatas of Jan Pieterszoon Sweelinck', *Tijdschrift van de Vereniging voor Nederlandse Muziekgeschiedemis* 25/2, (1975), 44–6 and 54–60.

13. Ibid., p. 47.

14. Only the first four-part statement of the melody of 'Allein Gott in der Höh sei Ehr' (A1) could have been headed 'Theme'. It presents the tune in the treble, supported throughout by chords with passing notes, not unlike Bach's vocal settings. Yet the piece is termed 'Variatio'.

15. Sigtenhorst Meyer, *Jan P. Sweelinck en zijn instrumentale muziek*, pp.194 ff.

16. See the Bibliography in *Opera omnia*, i, nos. 50 and 51.

17. This manuscript has been published in A. Curtis (ed.) *Monumenta Musica Neerlandica*, iii, (Amsterdam, 1961).

18. For practical reasons the fragment from the Susanne van Soldt Manuscript has been transposed up a major second.

19. This concluding section is based on the English and Polish versions of the author's *Forma formans*, (Amsterdam, 1969). See Select Bibliography for details.

20. L. B. Alberti, *De pictura praestantissima et nunquam satis laudata arte libri tres* (Basle, 1540), Liber II, 73.

21. C. van Mander, *Den Grondt der Edel vry Schilderkonst* (Alkmaar, 1604), 20–2, 26 and 33.

22. J. Tinctoris, *Liber de arte contrapuncti*, iii, cap. VIII. See C.-E.-H. de Coussemaker, *Scriptorum de musica medii aevi nova series a Gerbertina altera*, iv, 152, (Paris, 1864–76).

CHAPTER V

1. Van Noordt's *Tabulatuur-Boeck* appeared in a new edition by Jan van Biezen in *Monumenta Musica Neerlandica*, xi, (Amsterdam, 1976).

2. See F. R. Noske (ed.) *Monumenta Musica Neerlandica*, xvi, (Amsterdam, 1985).

SELECT BIBLIOGRAPHY

COMPLETE EDITIONS

A. *Works* (The Hague-Leipzig 1894–1901), 10 vols. (i–ix ed. M. Seiffert; x ed. H. Gehrmann).

    i   *Works for Organ and Harpsichord* (re-edited and largely extended: Amsterdam, 1943; Supplement, ed. A. Annegarn: Amsterdam, 1958).

  ii–v *Psalms* (four books).

  vi *Cantiones sacrae.*

  vii *Chansons.*

 viii *Rimes françoises et italiennes.*

  ix *Miscellaneous Works.*

  x *Rules of Composition.*

B. *Opera omnia* (Amsterdam, 1957—)

   i *The Instrumental Works* (1968).

     Fasc. 1, *Keyboard Works: Fantasias and Toccatas*, ed. G. Leonhardt.

     Fasc. 2, *Keyboard Works: Settings of Sacred Melodies*, ed. A. Annegarn.

     Fasc. 3, *Keyboard Works: Settings of Secular Melodies and Dances; Works for Lute*, ed. F. Noske.

   ii *Cinquante pseaumes de David*, ed. R. Lagas (1965).

  iii *Livre second des pseaumes de David*, ed. R. Lagas (1966).

  iv *Livre troisiesme des pseaumes de David* (two fascicles), ed. C. Maas (1981).

   v *Livre quatriesme des pseaumes de David*, edd. J. van Biezen and R. Tollefsen (to be published in 1988).

  vi *Cantiones sacrae*, ed. B. van den Sigtenhorst Meyer (1957); rev.A. Annegarn (1979).

  vii *Secular Vocal Works; Miscellaneous Vocal Works*, ed. A. Verhoeven-Kooij (in preparation).

LITERATURE

Note: A comprehensive list of scholarly editions and literature about Sweelinck's instrumental works up till 1968 is included in each of the three fascicles of the *Opera omnia*, vol. i.

BORREN, C. VAN DEN, 'Quelques notes sur les chansons françaises et les madrigaux italiens de J. P. Sweelinck', *Gedenkboek aangeboden aan Dr D. F. Scheurleer* (The Hague, 1925), 73–87.

BRADSHAW, M. C., 'The Toccatas of Jan Pieterszoon Sweelinck', *Tijdschrift van de Vereniging voor Nederlandse Muziekgeschiedenis* 25/2, (1975) 38–60.

BREIG, W., 'Der Umfang des choralgebundeten Orgelwerks von Jan Pieterszoon Sweelinck', *Archiv für Musikwissenschaft*, 17 (1960), 258–76.

CURTIS, A., *Sweelinck's Keyboard Music: A Study of English Elements in Seventeenth-Century Dutch Composition* (Leiden and London, 1969).

GERDES, G., *Die Choralvariationen J. P. Sweelincks und seiner Schüler*, Dissertation, University of Freiburg, 1956.

MISCHIATI, O., 'L'intavolatura d'organo tedesca della Biblioteca Nazionale di Torino', *L'Organo*, 4 (1963), pp. 1–154.

NOSKE, F. R., *Forma formans, Een structuuranalytische methode, toegepast op de instrumentale muziek van Jan Pieterszoon Sweelinck* (Amsterdam, 1969). Revised English edn. in *International Review of the Aesthetics and Sociology of Music*, 7 (1976), pp. 43–62. Polish transl. in *Res facta*, 9 (1982), pp. 214–29.

——, 'Remarques sur les luthistes des Pays-Pas (1580–1620)', *Le luth et sa musique*, ed. J. Jacquot (Neuilly-sur-Seine, 1957), pp. 179–92.

SCHIERNING, L., *Die Überlieferung der deutschen Orgel- und Klaviermusik aus der ersten Hälfte des 17. Jahrhunderts* (Kassel, 1961).

SIGTENHORST MEYER, B. VAN DEN, *Jan P. Sweelinck en zijn instrumentale muziek*, 2nd rev. edn. (The Hague, 1946).

——, *De vocale muziek van Jan P. Sweelinck* (The Hague, 1948).

TOLLEFSEN, R. H., 'Jan Pietersz. Sweelinck: A Bio-Bibliography', *Tijdschrift van de Vereniging voor Nederlandse Muziekgeschiedenis*, 22/2, (1971) pp. 87–125.

TUSLER, R. L., *The Organ Music of Jan Pieterszoon Sweelinck* (Bilthoven, 1958).

VOIGTS, A., 'Die Toccaten Jan Pieterszoon Sweelincks', unpublished dissertation, University of Münster, 1955.

INDEX

139

140

141